GUNS
OF THE
WILD WEST

TEXT BY
DAVID KENNEDY
CURATOR, THE CODY FIREARMS MUSEUM
THE BUFFALO BILL HISTORICAL CENTER

PHOTOGRAPHY BY
BRUCE CURTIS

Konecky & Konecky
72 Ayers Point Rd.
Old Saybrook, CT 06475
Visit us on the web!
www.koneckyandkonecky.com

This edition published by arrangement with The Perseus Books Group

10 digit ISBN 1-56852-788-8
13 digit ISBN 978-1-56852-788-8

Cover and interior design by Doogie Horner
Edited by Lisa Clancy
Typography: Acmefont, Goudy, Birch, Blackoak, Bodoni, Bodoni Highlight, Bookman, Cottonwood, Egyptienne, Juniper, Madrone, Mesquite, Ponderosa, Poplar, Rockwell, Willow, Woodtype Ornaments

Printed and bound in India by Replika Press Pvt. Ltd.

CARL LAEMMLE, OFFERS
WALCAMP
CODY RIDES WILD
ONE OF THE FAMOUS
SADDLE" STORIES
DIRECTED BY JACQUES JACCARD
REWARD
($500.00)
Reward for the capture, dead or alive,
of one Wm. Bonney better known as
"BILLY THE KID"
"BUFFALO BILL"

TABLE OF CONTENTS

PART 1
THE EXPLORATION OF THE WEST

PART 2
WAR AND EXPANSION

PART 3
"CIVILIZING" THE WEST

PART 4
WORKING AND FIGHTING

PART 5
FIREARMS OF DISTINCTION

PART 6
REPRESENTATIONS OF THE WEST

THE CHANGING AND NEW WEST

Guns and the history of the American West go hand in hand, both in fact and in fantasy. The stories have been told and retold, and have become an inherent part of American society. In order to understand much of the nation's psychology and history, it is necessary to understand the cowboy, the sodbuster, the soldier, the prostitute, the trapper, the businessman, and the hunter. Despite the protestations of some, the vast majority of those people living in the West carried firearms at one time or another. This relationship is still strong in the West, whether inspiring or resulting from the independent spirit of the region and the story that came from it. What you are about to read is a small attempt to help you understand that story

Although you have probably already skipped this part of the book and started elsewhere, I think I should mention a few things about the book in your hands. As a "gun guy," I have seen more than my share of gun books aimed (no pun intended) at those who collect and/or shoot regularly. The market is not lacking in books of this type. However, I believe there is a need for gun books that will be enjoyed by those who are simply interested in the gun's role in our history and are not worried about whether or not they will gain an encyclopedic understanding of the subject matter. During my tenure at the Cody Firearms Museum, I have met many people who could care less about the caliber, the technical specifications, or the numbers produced of a certain gun than they do about how it was used and by whom. To this end I will not go into a lot of "gun guy" detail unless it aids the story. If this book piques your interest to learn more of the story of Firearms and the American West, please look at the firearms bibliography at the end. The volumes referenced there will teach you more about guns than I could attempt to in a book this size.

For all of you gun guys who are now frowning, don't worry, you'll find some things that you will enjoy and even a few things that you will want to holler at. While most of what you read here is well-documented fact, there is a lot based on hearsay, legends, campfire stories, and even downright lies. For most stories of the West and its guns, there are several versions, depending on the source. Where guns are concerned, there are occasional disputes regarding aspects of historical production and use. In these cases I went with the interpretation I felt to be more accurate. This is not the ultimate source of information on the subject of guns used in the West, nor is it meant to be. Again, I would refer those looking for more information to the books listed in the bibliography.

A few comments on terminology are in order. For the gun terms, I am going with those I usually employ. I know that within certain quarters, some of the terminology is a bit different and quite convoluted. For example, I expect to receive numerous letters decrying my description of the Ohio rifle described within as an "American Long Rifle." In these cases I am choosing to go with the term that I feel best presents the story to the reader who is new to the subject. If you dislike the terminology I use, please remember that there are folks who do not know the story yet. Attempting to provide encyclopedic information is, as I have said, out of the scope of

this book and would only confuse those who are learning some of this for the first time. As a related note, the reader will note a tendency to use masculine pronouns (he, him, and his) and generic terms (salesmen). This is not an attempt to dismiss the role of women in the West or express some sense of gender bias, but rather to maintain a level of historical accuracy. Those cases in which it is appropriate to mention women with guns will receive the proper treatment. Famous women with guns were the exception, not the rule. This situation can only be corrected if research shows this statement to be wrong.

I would like to thank the staff of Running Press, especially my editor, Lisa Clancy, for putting up with my continual blowing of deadlines. Bruce, thank you for showing me the ropes. Bob Pickering and Chuck Preston for the lessons taught during the writing of this book. To the ladies of the Pony Expresso (my other office), thanks for all of the caffeine. Bob and Warren, Liz and Ann Marie, Connie and Gary and the rest of the staff at the BBHC, thanks for the support and help around the CFM. Thanks to my dad for teaching me about the West and to Heidi's dad for showing it to me. Lastly, thanks to my wife, Heidi, for putting up with my nonsense and procrastination during the writing of this book—and then putting up with more of the same from Jordan upon his arrival halfway through the process. Like father, like son.

I hope you enjoy this book half as much as I did writing it. The next time you happen to be in Cody, feel free to stop by to have it signed.

David Kennedy
Cody, Wyoming
March 2005

PART
I

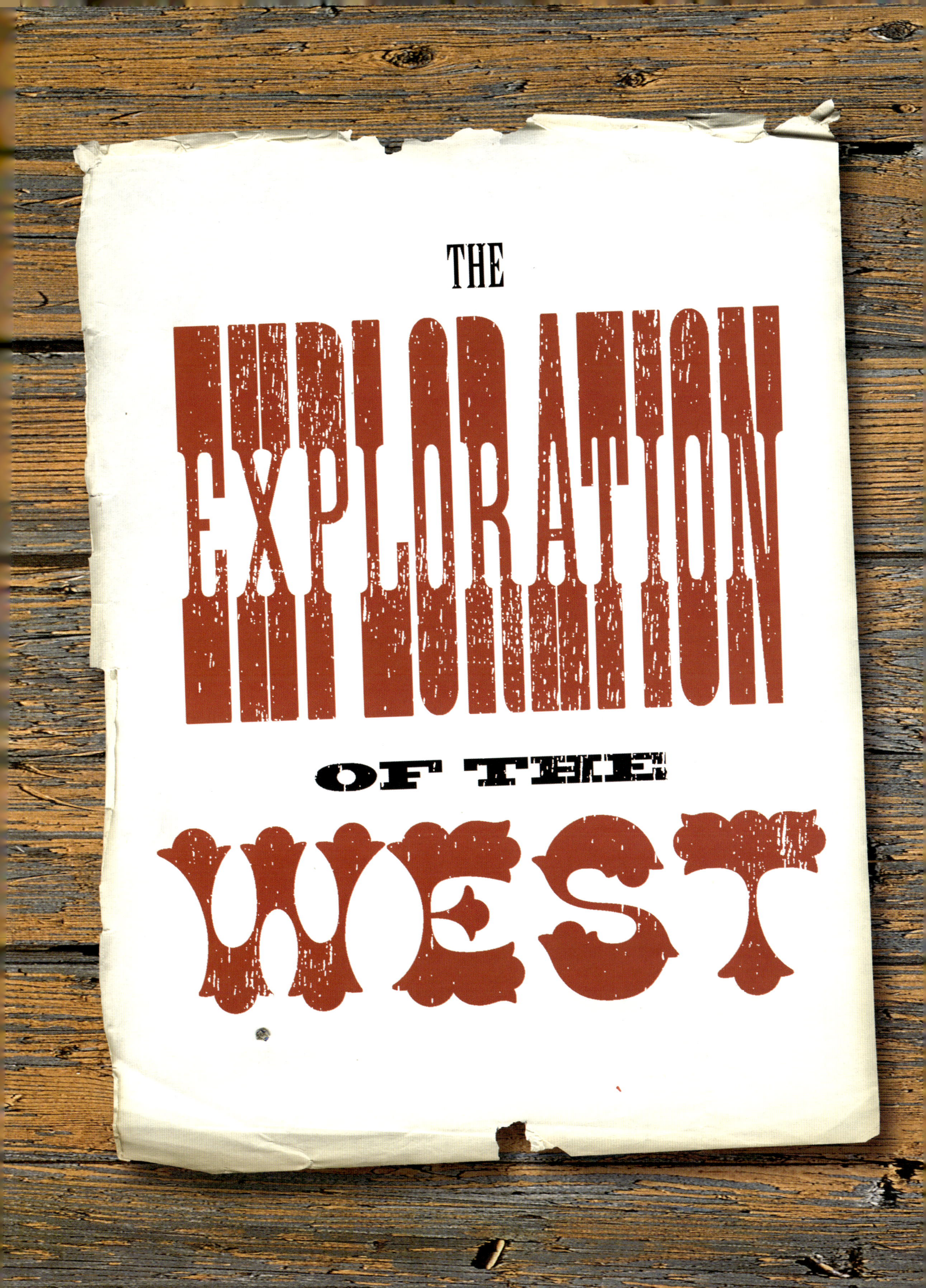
THE
EXPLORATION
OF THE
WEST

AMERICA'S FIRST ART

THE AMERICAN LONG RIFLE

Depending on the source, the definition of the West will change from person to person. Everyone understands the West to be a slightly different thing. Some people say it has been a geographical region. Others see it as being a frame of mind or a period of time. This view also depends on the time in which the person lives or lived. At one point the West was seen as the area of the Ohio River valley. Even earlier it was anything west of the Adirondack Mountains.

Over a 100-year period there was one particular style of firearm prevalent across the United States. The Minutemen and the fledgling Army of the United States carried this firearm. The earliest explorers into western Pennsylvania and past the Cumberland Gap carried this rifle. Daniel Boone, Davy Crockett, and Andrew Jackson and his troops at the Battle of New Orleans all used it. As the first truly original American art form, the American Long Rifle took the typically heavy European rifles imported in the 1700s and made a variety of design changes to improve them for use in the American Colonies.

The starting point of American arms design was the military-based flintlock arms in common use in Europe. These guns were large-caliber, heavy-barreled, short smoothbores that could be very effective at close range. As most of the arms in use in Europe during the 1700s were military in origin, the few civilian guns available had a similar appearance and style. While the use of rifling was well known and

American Long Rifle of the Ohio School, made by Peter Kane

American Long Rifle of the Ohio School, made by Peter Kane

understood as a construction element, the military preferred smoothbore arms to save money during construction and time on the battlefield. The bore, generally about .75 caliber—larger than a modern 12-gauge shotgun—was a side effect of the belief that bigger was better. The stock was often heavy, as well. In military terms, this made sense as many people considered the musket, with bayonet attached, to be a spear that could fire several shots before engaging the enemy in hand-to-hand combat. The only real difference between the European military and civilian arms was the length. While the military arms were generally longer at 5' to 6', the civilian arms were shorter, in the area of 4' in length. Presumably this would have been to lighten the gun. It merely made both the accuracy and the recoil worse.

There were many social, geographical, and, for lack of a better term, agricultural differences between Europe and the American Colonies. Being one of the far-flung Frontiers of Europe, the Colonies were on the edge of wilderness. Society not only allowed civilian firearm ownership, but *supported* it. There was an expectation, and often a legal requirement, that adult males were to be part of the village militia for defense against Indians and the French (or in the Canadian Colonies' case, Indians and the British). The local authorities went so far as to supply arms to those colonists who could not afford their own. The majority of the population lived in rural areas that were a long trip over terrain from a population center. Combined with the need to be self-sufficient regarding food production, this remoteness resulted in the need for a

MOST SCHOLARS CREDIT THE SKILLED ARTISANS OF LANCASTER COUNTY,PENNSYLVANIA, AS THE DEVELOPERS OF THE EARLIEST VERSION OF THE AMERICAN LONG RIFLE.

firearm with the dual purpose of hunting for food and defending livestock against predators. With all of these differences from the relatively gun- and hazard-free environment of Europe, it is not strange that a new rifle, one suited to the local situation, would be developed in the American Colonies.

Most scholars credit the skilled artisans of Lancaster County, Pennsylvania, as the developers of the earliest version of the American Long Rifle. Comprised primarily of German immigrants, Lancaster was a haven of craftsmen representing fine metal work, wood carving, and other industrial arts. These artisans were familiar with the manufacture of firearms for military and civilian use, and applied this knowledge to their new environment. With less importance on the speed of reloading and more importance for greater accuracy, the barrels were rifled. As accuracy improved, the size of the bullet decreased to an average of .45 caliber. Being lengthened from 30" to 40+" on average, also modified the barrel. These changes reduced the amount of metal needed, thus reducing the weight of the gun. Because no one expected this rifle to be used in a melee of any sorts, the stock could be much lighter, built strong enough to only support the barrel and action. The resulting firearm was light enough to be carried for miles and accurate enough to guarantee that the hunter would fill his pot.

Unlike the guns of today—or of the "Wild West" for that matter—this information is very much a generalization, as the individual arms produced from the various makers were exactly that—individual. Each gun, even by the same smith, was different. Regional and period changes were even greater. Scholarship over the last half century has shown how these guns differed by, and sometimes within, colony (later, state) and county. The biggest differences were between the "Pennsylvania" rifles and the "Kentucky" or "Tennessee" rifles. These differences in caliber, length, and stock shape were a result of the different needs of the settlers who had passed the Cumberland Gap. These changes also lead to the largest issue of this topic—the terminology used to discuss these arms. Many fans of these long guns will take part in very heated discussions as to the correct name of this type. In response to this, and in recognition of the importance of these arms in American history, the author prefers to stick with the all-encompassing term "American Long Rifle."

American Long Rifle of the Ohio School, made by Peter Kane

Girandoni Repeating Air Rifle, made by Ivan Polin, Tula, Russia

POSSIBILITIES OF DISCOVERY

EARLY AIR RIFLES

When the term “Air Rifle” is mentioned, most people (depending on their age) think of the names Red Ryder, Daisy, or Crossman. The mental image is that of a father teaching his child how to shoot a rifle safely or of that child traipsing through the woods with an air rifle, pretending to be an explorer in the West. Neither parent nor child realizes that Captains Meriwether Lewis and William Clark were equipped with a similar arm two centuries previously. While these images and the common understanding of air rifles are of recent creation, the reality of the air rifle is that it is not a product of the 20th century, but of the 18th century.

In the 1600s European gunmakers and scientists understood the effects of varying the pressure of air in a closed chamber, whether to compress it or to create a vacuum. A presumed step in this research was to investigate how a carefully released overpressure could propel objects in the manner that exploding black powder would when firing a gun. As a result of these experiments, several designers developed arms that could utilize air instead of requiring black powder and flints.

This development was used by a number of European armies to equip at least a small number of their soldiers. Most of these rifles would be bored for a .45 caliber ball or larger. The Austrian Army equipped a battalion of riflemen with .44 caliber air rifles. This weapon allowed them to operate in any weather and without the need to be resupplied with black powder. However, the complexity and expense of this arm combined with the unfortunate ability of the average soldier to break mechanical tools led to the end of this arm in widespread military service.

SEEN FROM THE TOP Girandoni Repeating Air Rifle, made by Ivan Polin, Tula, Russia

When equipping the Corps of Discovery, Captain Lewis decided to bring an air rifle along with the complement of black powder arms standard to any exploration of the period, military or otherwise. While this particular arm was still seen as being experimental by some, Lewis saw it as a valid choice due to the differences between it and the black powder arms in the inventory.

The decision was based on survival. Used in flintlock firearms, black powder becomes impossible to shoot in rainy weather. In percussion firearms, inclement weather greatly hinders the use of black powder. The primary cause of this is that black powder breaks down into its component parts in water. The inability to either provide for or defend yourself would, presumably, be rather important if you were out of contact with society.

The Corps of Discovery was expected to be in the wilderness for at least two years. If the Corps' supply of black powder were to get wet, due to weather or a soaking in the Missouri River, their primary weapons would be useless. (Lewis did develop an ingenious method for storing the black powder: using lead cans that could separately be melted down to produce bullets.)

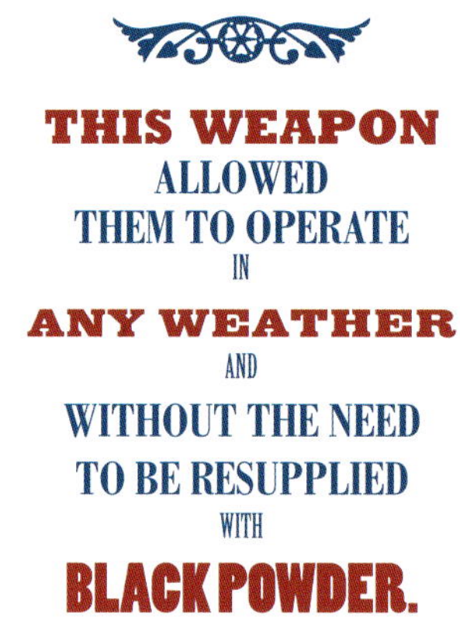

The actual gun used by the Corps was rarely mentioned in the various journals from the trip. There is agreement that it was a reasonably large caliber—.50 to .69. However, this is where agreement ends. For many years the only view has been that either Isaiah Lukens or his father, Seneca, both of Philadelphia, manufactured the appropriate arm. This was based primarily on the existence of an entry in Isaiah Luken's estate referring to a gun in his possession as being the air gun carried by Lewis and Clark in their exploration of the West. More research on this subject by Dr. Robert Beeman, considered by many to be the authority on air rifles, has added to this evidence.

Recent scholarship has brought some questioning to this theory. This scholarship involves the discovery of the journal of a British explorer who encountered the Corps of

Discovery as they headed west down the Ohio River. This entry appears to refer to a repeating rifle, not a single shot rifle of the Lukens type. This would seem to indicate the use of a rifle designed by Bartolomeo Girandoni, of Vienna. The Girandoni rifle has a magazine tube mounted coaxially, with a barrel using a spring and breechblock to allow the shooter to easily and quickly load the gun.

While this discussion is taken quite personally by some and the issue may never be resolved, it remains that Lewis and Clark did take an air rifle on their exploration. This firearm, while not having great importance in the later development of the West, did make its mark as a chosen tool of the first major expedition to the West. Similarly, the later air guns of the 20th century allowed several generations of American youth to play that they were with Lewis and Clark, carrying their important firearm on their own "adventures", even in their own back yards.

SIGNS OF ECONOMY

TRADE MUSKETS

One of the little discussed side effects of the industrial revolution is the change introduced to the indigenous peoples of the Americas. With the appearance of Europeans on the shores of the "New World," stone age cultures (and some with leanings toward the Iron Age) faced technologies they could not comprehend or overcome. As the Spanish, Portuguese, French, and English came to explore the American continents, their technology (and diseases) presented an unstoppable force. The many native cultures of the Americas eventually bent to the will of the invaders, sometimes by choice, other times not. The course of events differed from people to people and from country to country. While the Spanish and Portuguese used their technology in most cases to oppress the Inca, Aztec, and other peoples, the English and the French took a different route, for the most part.

Based in the different causes and philosophies behind the emigration to/invasion of the Americas, the relationship of the English and French to those already living in Columbus' "discovery" was more of a commercial interest than the military and religious mission of those from the Iberian Peninsula. The accepted reasons for the European exploration of Central

Flintlock Trade Musket common to the fur trade

AT THE BATTLE OF THE **LITTLE BIG HORN** CUSTER WAS FACED PRIMARILY BY **TRADE MUSKETS** AND BOWS.

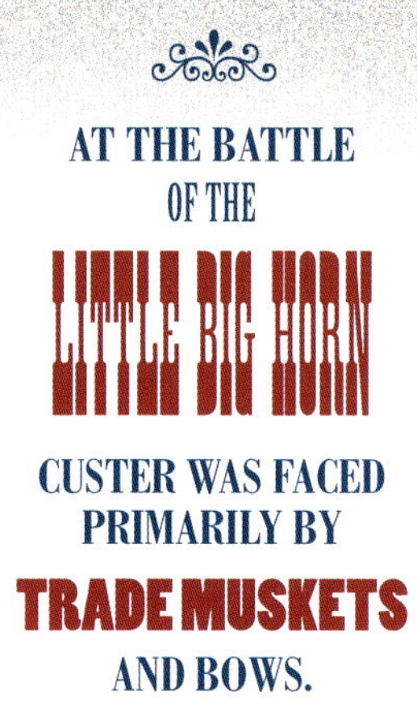

and South America were "God, Gold, and Glory." The ability to extract the second of this list–gold–from stationary locations while using stable trade routes for shipment enabled the Spanish, in particular, to centralize their operations. This centralization, in turn, helped the Spanish to maintain control of the territories they possessed.

In the regions that would one day become the United States and Canada, the situation was much different. Instead of fixed sources of gold, there were entire forests and animals spread across many hundreds and thousands of miles. With wide tracts of wilderness, a lack of centralized natural resources, and few, if any, established trade corridors, the French and English who came to the Americas quickly developed a series of trade networks that crisscrossed the continent. The basis of this trade network was to co-opt the various tribes in each region, rather than subjugate them.

The key to this network was the presence of European manufactured goods. Despite the many stories of Europeans duping Indians with "beads and trinkets," most of the trade goods supplied were of a less decorative nature. Made primarily of iron and steel, the goods were generally of a sturdy, utilitarian nature: pots, knives, hatchets, steel strikers for

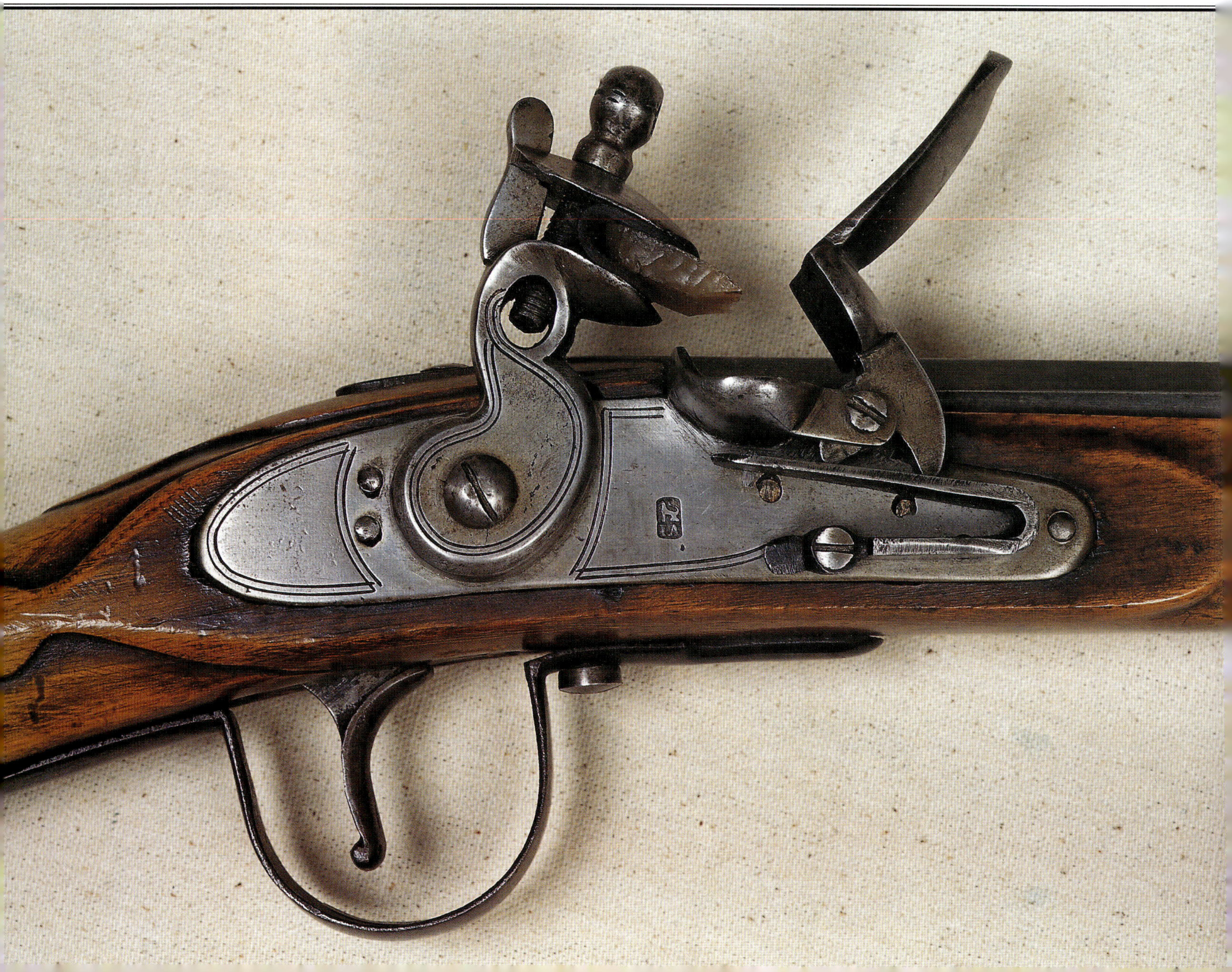

Flintlock Trade Musket with visible "Tombstone Fox" proofmark

starting fires, and, firearms. Traded to the Indians by the Hudson's Bay Company in the northern Rockies and Great Plains, and a variety of independent traders and pelt companies to the south of that, the manufactured goods eventually replaced handmade products within the Plains and Rocky Mountain cultures. This change created a dependence on these goods in many areas. As the trade in beaver pelts shifted to buffalo tongues and, later, buffalo hides, these manufactured goods both created a dependency and drastically affected the ecosystem and culture of the Great Plains and Rocky Mountains.

One of the more highly desired of these trade goods was the firearm. Typically this would be a large-caliber, crudely built flintlock, manufactured in Europe and shipped to the colonies as one of many trade goods. The trade musket took and held an early lead as the most widely used firearm among the Native American population. At the Battle of the Little Big Horn—decades after the development of the percussion cap and of the metallic cartridge—Lieutenant Colonel George Armstrong Custer was faced primarily by trade muskets and bows, not Winchester Model 1866s, Model 1873s, or other repeaters as has been commonly told.

The most desired of the trade muskets, especially in the Northern Plains and Rockies had a stamp of a sitting dog in a tombstone- or circle-shaped outline. Named after the proof mark used, the guns provided by the Hudson's Bay Company were deemed the most reliable of the various trade guns. The mere presence of this mark conferred a greater value on the gun in question. The trade musket pictured here, manufactured by W. L. Sargent of London, has the tombstone fox.

Regardless of the proof mark, the trade musket was a symbol of social standing, power, and authority from the 18th to the turn of the 20th century. On the downside, the owner of such an arm was dependent on the European traders for black powder and lead, creating a superior/subordinate relationship that allowed the traders, whether French or English, Canadian or American, to control the trade and, by extension, the region. This power relationship consistently kept the American Indian in a decidedly poor position when trading or making any agreements with the White traders with whom they dealt.

THE ARMY'S STANDARD

THE US MODEL 1803

A constant of national expansion for any country is soldiers on the frontier. Whether a European border or the wilderness beyond the Allegheny Mountains, the militaries of many nations have been responsible for guarding the frontier from an enemy army, preventing the populace from emigrating, or maintaining a "peace" in the absence of any semblance of government. These soldiers, if they were lucky, would receive the best and newest weapons and equipment. The American Army in the early 1800s was often armed with some of the best military arms in the world.

As previously mentioned, in 1803 a small detachment of soldiers left Philadelphia and headed west. This group, led by Captains Meriwether Lewis and William Clark, was the first government-sponsored expedition into the area of the Louisiana Territory. The discoveries made and maps created by this expedition were invaluable to those who followed later. During the period of the Corps of Discovery's travels to the Pacific and back, they represented the largest detachment of the American military beyond St. Louis. Elsewhere in the United States small outposts of soldiers were salted throughout the Ohio River Valley and the inhabited portions of the South.

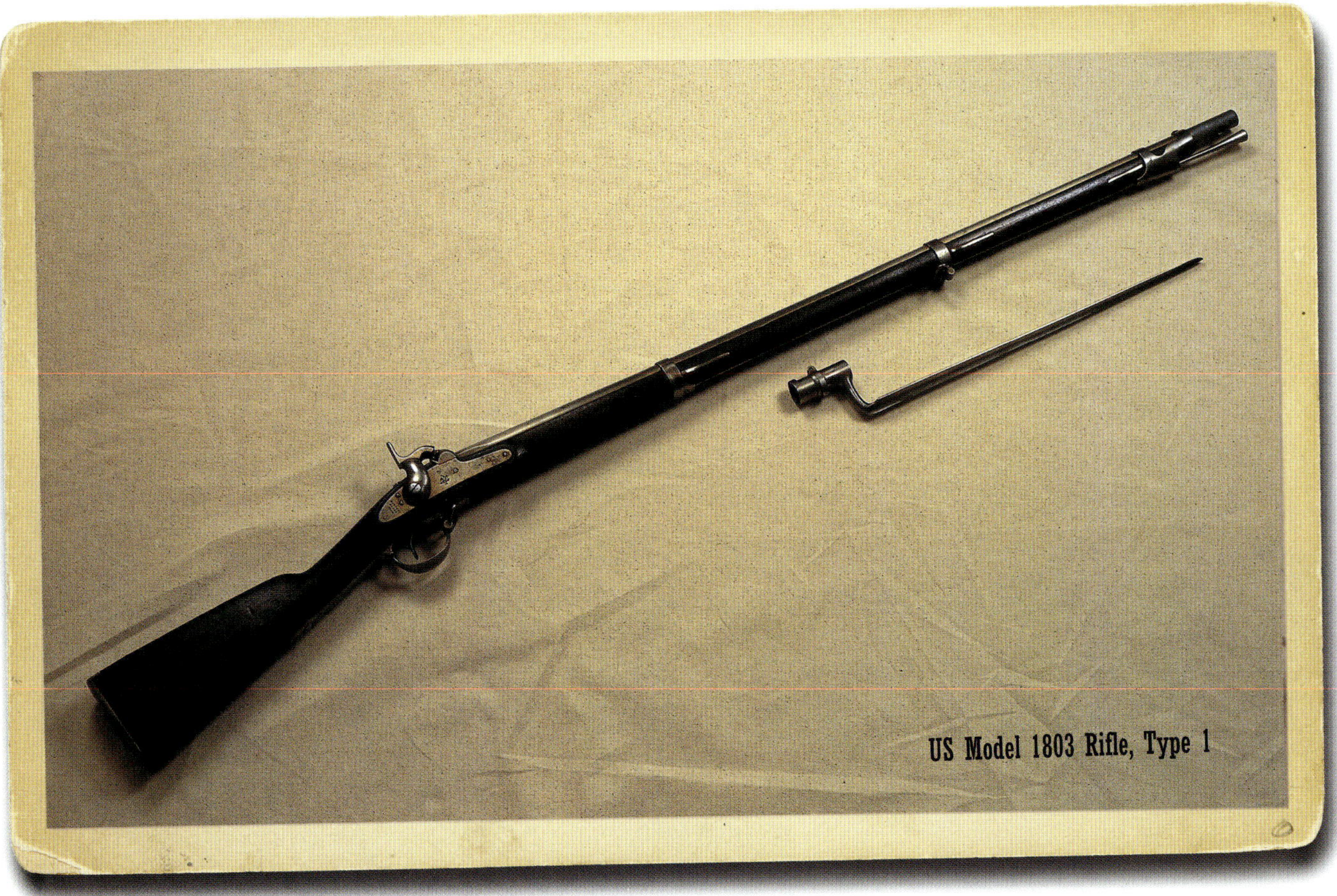
US Model 1803 Rifle, Type 1

The arms normally issued to these soldiers were variations on the Charleville Pattern Musket, a gun often incorrectly referred to as the US Model 1795. The Charleville Pattern Musket was a .69 caliber smoothbore flintlock based on the French Model 1763, the most commonly found arm in the Continental Army of the American Revolution. Between the introduction of the Charleville pattern in 1795 and the end of the War of 1812, the American Army issued approximately 150,000 arsenal-built arms. Small contractors built untold thousands of arms of the same model to arm various militia organizations and privateers. A secondary arm issued to rifle companies was the US Contract Rifle, manufactured from 1792 to 1809. Built in small shops in Pennsylvania, this was the first rifle adopted by the fledgling nation. This model of rifle, with some modifications, is believed to be the model carried by Lewis and Clark and the few soldiers who were with them on their departure from Philadelphia.

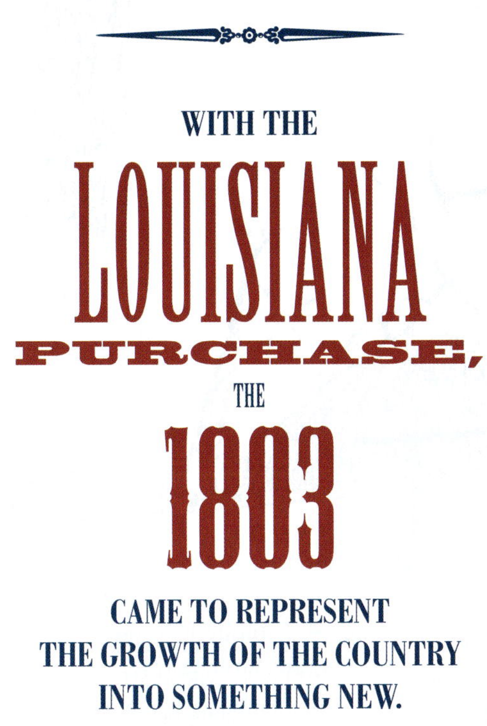

During the years leading up to the Corp's expedition to the West, the Department of War began preparations for the introduction of a new standard rifle. As a result of the many variations of caliber and construction in the Contract Rifle of 1792 and the occasionally questionable condition of civilian rifles used by riflemen in federal service, there was a need for a standardized rifle. Standardization would lower production cost and smooth out any issues of supply. One commonly accepted story is that the design originated from elements of the Contract Rifle with modifications made at the suggestion of Meriwether Lewis. This model, introduced at the Harper's Ferry Arsenal in 1803, was the common rifled longarm for 15 years, with almost 20,000 arms constructed over that period.

This rifle was important in the development of military arms in several ways. It was the first standardized rifle to be adopted by the American military. Additionally it was the first American military arm designed entirely within our borders. The design, essentially an evolution of the American Long Rifle, was vastly different from any other military arm in use at the time. With a light half-stock and smooth lines, the soldiers who carried it appreciated the appearance and weight. Oddly, for all of the positive points of this rifle, the subsequent rifles that followed in the country's service followed the "normal" design philosophy of constructing arms with full, stout stocks, making the arms heavier than necessary, but conforming to standard design concepts.

For many years it was believed that this model was the firearm carried by Lewis and Clark. After a number of years of research and the application of logic regarding the timeframe of the expedition, many historians have reached the conclusion that the 1803 were simply manufactured too late to be part of the equipment for the trip to the Pacific. Regardless, the 1803 did receive its share of use. It was the standard rifle of the War of 1812 and many soldiers stationed in what was once the West, both when it was east and west of the Mississippi River, carried this rifle.

With the Louisiana Purchase, which occurred the same year as the rifle was introduced, the 1803 came to represent the growth of the country into something new. With the vibrancy of the national spirit and the quick expansion of the nation's borders, the 1803 came to be used across the nation and on the frontier as a supporting weapon to the Charleville Pattern Musket. The pairing of these two arms, each a world-class arm in its own right, put the new military on par with the rest of the world. Combined with the desire to protect the nation and the urge to see the frontier, the soldiers who carried these arms were well supplied in their efforts. Whether the West was in Ohio River Valley, the Mississippi River Valley, or the new area of the Louisiana Purchase, this gun helped defend it and support those who wanted to live there.

BIG GUNS TO THE MOUNTAINS

THE HAWKEN RIFLE

The Hawken rifle is seen by many as being the stereotypical firearm of the mountain man. An image comes to mind of a grizzled man with a full beard, animal skins for clothing, one or more single-shot percussion pistols tucked away, and a Green River knife strapped to his side. The mountain man may have a horse or mule as a pack animal, but will more often than not have all of his belongings on him or in his camp. However, his most important belonging was his rifle. Made in St. Louis, the heavy rifle of the fur trade era was the signifying weapon of the period.

This rifle had Hawken stamped on it somewhere. However, when most people say "Hawken", they are often referring to what is more correctly called a Plains Rifle. While the Hawken brothers may have developed the style of rifle, they were not the only manufacturers of this rifle.

The city of St. Louis was the step-off point for many of the trappers, traders, scouts, and other adventurers who went into the West. These travelers, originally arriving from the East with their American Long Rifles manufactured in Pennsylvania and Kentucky, soon realized that the firearms they brought were inadequate to the task of surviving in the wilderness. The American Long Rifle was perfect for life in the East. It was light, very accurate, and easy to care for. However, it was also intended for use in the field during the day and a spot above the mantle in the evening. The accuracy was, in part, due to the length of the barrel—5 feet or more in some cases. It was also designed primarily to shoot at small game, not deer, elk, or bison.

Hawken Rifle owned by John Johnston,
A/K/A Jeremiah Johnson or "Liver Eating" Johnson

The Plains Rifle was designed to overcome these inadequacies. The new gun was shorter, sturdier in the stock, and larger in caliber. All of these changes helped the rifle to survive rough handling and mistreatment in the wild while being able to work more effectively as a hunting tool. The accuracy was more than capable to take down game when encountered at distances of 50 yards or less—not a hard task when the game animals had not experienced many humans. The weight and stoutness of the gun came into use if the gun was relegated to the role of a club. While the typical American Long Rifle's smooth lines and light weight may have aided in its role as a short-trip hunting rifle, it would have been reduced to kindling if used in this manner.

THE NEW GUN WAS **SHORTER, STURDIER** IN THE STOCK, AND **LARGER** IN CALIBER.

One key difference between these two guns was an increase in weight. With a larger caliber came larger barrels, made with even thicker walls in order to increase the sturdiness of the rifles and durability with large caliber bullets. Even by shortening the barrels, this would increase the overall weight of the arm. Some of the heaviest rifles of this type weighed in at just under twenty pounds. The rifle pictured in this section is an example of a heavier Hawken. Bored for a .50 caliber ball, the 32" long barrel is 1 ½" in diameter. The overall weight is 13 ½ pounds, heavy enough to help stabilize the rifle while aiming and reduce the recoil to almost nothing. While the rifle is not standard for the type, it does fit within the description of a Plains Rifle. It was manufactured by the originator of the style–Samuel Hawken. To make the history of this rifle more interesting, we have to look at the owner, one John "Liver-Eating" Johnston.

Known as Jeremiah Johnson in the public due in no small part to a film named after him, John Johnston was a trapper, scout, and occasional ne'er-do-well. Born in the 1820s, he traveled the West from Montana to California and everywhere in between. During his travels John Johnston entered into a blood feud with the entire Crow nation.

After the brutal murder of his wife–believed to be perpetrated by local Indians–Johnston went insane and set out to kill any Crow Indian he could find. According to the story, Johnston ate the liver of his prey, becoming more savage than Westerners mistakenly believed the Indians to be. Unfortunately there is little in the way of factual information regarding Johnston. However, there has been much written about him that is conjecture at best and complete fiction at worst.

The most popular book about Johnston, *Crow Killer*, has proven to be a popular read for almost a half century. While there are more than a few factual events cited by the authors, the majority of the book should be seen as a collection of stories about several unknown mountain men who lived during the period. Received by word-of-mouth, and second- and third-hand at that, the authors acknowledge at points that there was much confusion regarding Johnston. In an era before "Headline News", *The New York Times*, and the internet, it would have been difficult to definitively identify anyone—even a 6' 2" (some say 6' 6"), 250-pound giant of a man. If nothing else, *Crow Killer* raised Johnston to the level of Davy Crockett, Daniel Boone, and other mythic woodsmen in American history.

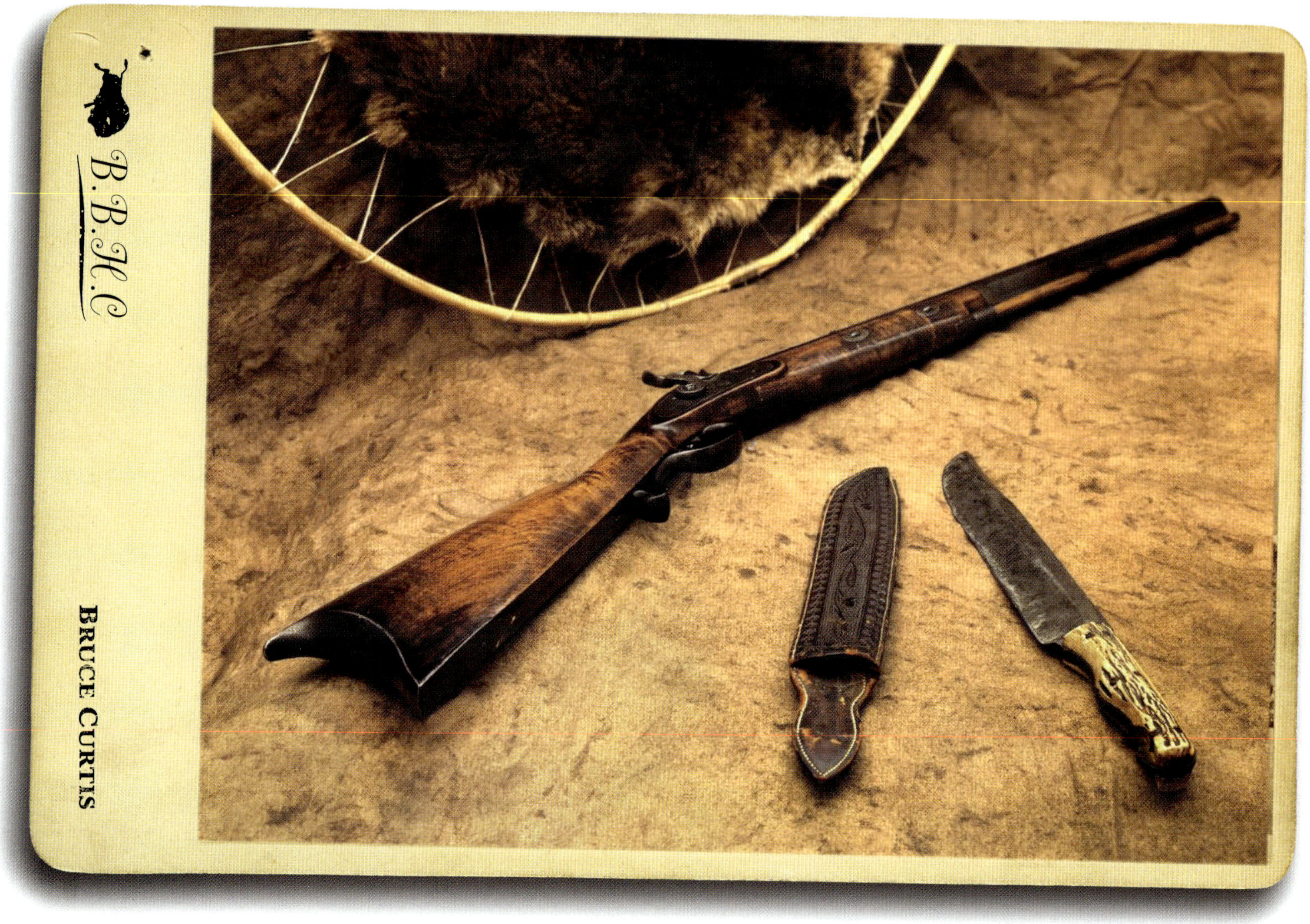

B.B.H.C
BRUCE CURTIS

Hawken Rifle owned by John Johnston, A/K/A Jeremiah Johnson or "Liver Eating" Johnson

JOHN JOHNSTON WAS A **TRAPPER, SCOUT,** AND OCCASIONAL **NE'ER-DO-WELL.**

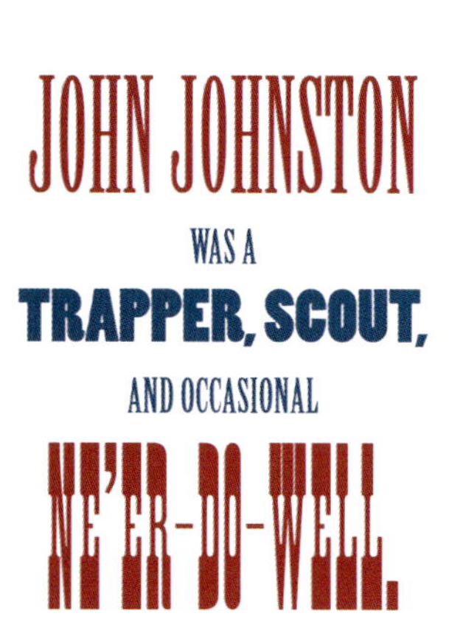

What is known is that Johnston was a typical Western jack-of-all-trades. He sold cordwood for a living, trapped for skins, fought as a soldier in the Civil War, went to war against the entirety of the Crow Nation, and served as a lawman. Known to have a vicious temper—some would say he was just mean—settlers and Indians alike would go out of their way to avoid upsetting the man. Eventually succumbing to old age, Johnston traveled to California where he spent his last months in the Los Angeles Old Soldiers Home. In December 1899, he entered the Veteran's Administration Hospital, dying the next month on January 21, 1900.

The story does not end there. As the result of renewed interest in Johnson's life, partially drummed up by the publication of *Crow Killer*, Warner Brothers released the film "Jeremiah Johnson" in 1972. Starring Robert Redford, this film built on Johnston's mythic status. During that same year, a movement to have Johnston's body returned to the region of the Rocky Mountains was finally successful. However, after being turned down by the town of Red Lodge, Montana—despite Johnston's tenure as sheriff for several years—the neighboring town of Cody, Wyoming, accepted the body for burial. This re-interment took place in 1974—allowing Warner Brothers to capitalize on the event by making sure that Redford was present at the ceremony. As for other aspects of Johnston's heritage, Red Lodge still has possession of the cabin that was Johnston's home while he lived there. As for the pictured gun, it resides in the Cody Firearms Museum with the associated knife, allowing many thousands of visitors to enjoy this story of the West.

CALAMITY JANE SEATED WITH A WINCHESTER MODEL 1873

PART
III

WAR
AND
EXPANSION

"Pepperbox"-style Pistols

SOMETIMES THEY ALL GO OFF...

PEPPERBOX PISTOLS

The common language of firearms in the West involves the names of Colt, Winchester, Remington, and Sharps, among others. While these famous manufacturers represent a large number of firearms seen in the hands of cowboys, lawmen, and criminals in the West, there were guns that preceded them in use. Not only did these guns show up in the West in large numbers before the "six-shooter," familiar to most people, but their introduction to the West also took place before many of the other "famous" guns of the West. Originally developed in Europe, the odd-looking firearms known as pepperboxes were at one time widespread in the West.

The most obvious mark of a pepperbox is the barrel-like cylinder and barrel assembly. Instead of being constructed of a fixed barrel and a revolving cylinder, like the later revolvers manufactured by Colt, Remington, and Smith & Wesson, the barrels and cylinders are one and the same. Developed in an era dominated by single-shot muzzle-loading pistols and rifles, pepperboxes were the next technological step. Effectively a multi-barrel, repeating muzzleloader, pepperboxes allowed the user to prepare a shot in each of the three to ten (but usually six) barrels. Although the early pepperboxes required the user to cock the gun manually, later models were capable of performing these actions with a single trigger pull—beating the widespread use of this design feature in revolvers by several decades.

"Pepperbox"-style Pistols

This change from single action to double action design was a result of the manufacturer Ethan Allen, responsible for many of the pepperboxes still found in circulation. Allen's various companies produced these guns for a thirty year period from the mid-1830s until 1865. One of the reasons behind the stability of Allen's production was his choice of business partners. From 1842 to 1847, Allen partnered with his brother-in-law, Charles Thurber. Following this, he set up a new corporation with another brother-in-law, T.P. Wheelock. On Wheelock's death in 1864, Allen brought his sons-in-law, Sullivan Forehand and Henry C. Wadsworth, into the fold. After Allen's death in 1871, these two individuals continued the company in their own name, and became quite successful in their own right. During the entirety of this period, Allen always employed capable workers who, thinking they could make something better, sometimes struck out on their own after cutting their

The artist Alexander Phimister Proctor posing with a Remington Rolling Block rifle and a Pepperbox Pistol

teeth with Allen. These individuals manufactured arms that were often based directly on Allen's designs and were often stamped 'Allen's Patent.' This mobility of key employees was a common thread within the industry—and still is today.

While the barrel length on many of these firearms mitigated the danger of a firing barrel igniting additionally barrels, the shorter-barreled models were occasionally known to fire the intended barrel, followed shortly thereafter by one or more of the remaining barrels. This situation came up in the John Wayne film "Rooster Cogburn" (Universal Pictures, 1975). The Duke, in handing a short pepperbox to the Indian boy, Wolf, warns him that sometimes one barrel will fire and sometimes they all fire. While the ability of these arms to fire six bullets in a short period of time could be very formidable, the possibility of all six barrels firing at once would probably seem akin to looking down the business end of a shotgun. This amount of firepower in a compact source, despite the increased cost and mechanical complexity over a simple muzzleloader, would probably be enough enticement for anyone in the West to purchase one for personal use, whether for offense or defense.

Many of the early owners of these guns were travelers heading to the Gold Rush in California. As time went along, the ownership moved to an urban population, as city dwellers often wanted a small gun that could provide lots of firepower. There was the additional benefit that they were reliable and inexpensive—$5 to $15 versus the $20 or more for a Colt. By the period of the Civil War, a new market grew as many Union officers carried these guns as a sidearm. However, as the increasing industrialization within the gun industry led a corresponding drop in price, the newer designs by Colt and others quickly overtook the market niche held by the pepperboxes.

THE POSSIBILITY OF ALL SIX BARRELS FIRING AT ONCE WOULD SEEM AKIN TO LOOKING DOWN THE BUSINESS END OF A SHOTGUN.

The place of the pepperbox in the history of the West has not received enough attention. A sturdy and reliable gun, the pepperbox was inexpensive and easily concealed. It served as a sidearm for many settlers, soldiers, and city dwellers. The need for Western citizens to own a means of defense allowed this design to fill a hole, literally and figuratively, for almost thirty years. Although the "Big Three" of Colt, Remington, and Smith & Wesson were manufacturing many fine arms during this period, the market price of their products was often twice and three times the price of similar pepperboxes. This fact alone explains in simple monetary reasons how this basic firearm can be seen as a democratic weapon, if you will, allowing all social classes the ability to protect themselves.

A CAPTAIN, A COMPANY, & A CONCEPT

THE COLT WALKER

One of the earliest and best-known American stories of a gun involves an entrepreneur from New York, a Texas Ranger, and not one, but two, wars. Additionally, this story gives an insight to the process of how events and people affect gun designs. The gun involved in this story is the Colt Walker, also known as the Walker Dragoon. Before the appearance of the .44 Magnum cartridge in 1955, it had been over a century since the previous record holder for sheer firepower was manufactured. This record holder, the Colt Walker, had a limited production run—only 1100 were made—and enjoyed a short life in use, but it is still the focus of conversations concerning the big guns of the West.

The entrepreneur involved in this story was Samuel Colt. One of the most famous men in world history, Sam Colt was the epitome of the entrepreneurial spirit. After traveling to India as a sailor, he went up and down the east coast as a snake oil salesman, peddling nitrous oxide in order to pay for the manufacturing of his guns. Starting in the 1830s he manufactured several models of his firearms in Paterson, New Jersey, and Hartford, Connecticut. Most of these guns can now be seen more as failures than successes. However, each attempt taught Colt a little more about his business.

In the early 1840s, Captain Samuel Walker, the aforementioned Texas Ranger and commander of Company C of the United States Mounted Riflemen, approached Colt with his ideas regarding a design that would better serve soldiers. One of the few men in the military who could speak with authority on Colt's firearms, Walker used an early Colt repeating percussion rifle while serving in the Seminole Wars in Florida. Impressed with the capabilities of these arms, but realizing their shortcomings, Walker felt he could make improvements. These improvements included increasing the size of the earlier, Paterson, New Jersey, made revolvers,

ABOVE Colt Walker Model Revolver
RIGHT Geronimo holding a Colt Dragoon Revolver

adding a fixed trigger guard, changing the design to use a .44 caliber conical bullet, and a chamber that could handle the equivalent of an oversized, or "Magnum", powder charge. The result of this was a hefty 4 pound, 9 ounce, piece of metal and wood that was, for its day, the largest repeating handgun available.

The creation of this revolver was timely. In 1846 the United States went to war with Mexico. The Walker, ordered originally for use by the US Dragoons (mounted riflemen), ended up with the Rangers. Texas now had the entire stock of 1000 guns. The Rangers then issued the guns by pairs among its five companies, with the individual rangers buying the guns outright or having the price deducted from their pay. Unfortunately for researchers and historians, there is no list of how the guns were ultimately issued, as they were effectively sold to private individuals. We do know that many of the Rangers took their Walkers to Mexico during the war.

The events in Mexico involving the Rangers are definitely the stuff from which legends are made. Heroics, victories, and tall tales abound, but there are some stories that are understood to be fact. At the Battle of Juamantla on October 9, 1847, the Rangers fought a numerically superior force of Mexican Lancers. This victory, credited by some to the use of the Walker, ensured its place in Western folklore. However, this victory also saw the fall of Captain Walker. Among the stories surrounding his death are that he was shot by a sniper, stabbed with a lance, and that other Rangers found his body surrounded by a pile of dead Mexican soldiers. In some reports he was found dying, in others, dead. His Walker revolvers—both empty—were still in his hands. One of this pair of guns is in the collection of the Wadsworth Atheneum in Hartford, Connecticut.

During the Mexican-American War, the mounted riflemen discovered the shortcomings of the Walker. Some Rangers had a tendency to load the individual chambers with too much powder, leading to bursting cylinders on over a fifth of the guns—hopefully the shooter kept his fingers intact. The largest problem with the Walker, at least from the perspective of a soldier, would most likely have been the weight. Carrying the paired revolvers in holsters slung over the pommel of a saddle would be nice, but the balance and sheer size of these guns warranted improvement. Regardless, there are good arguments that this gun succeeded in its task—as a large military handgun that could be used as a primary weapon.

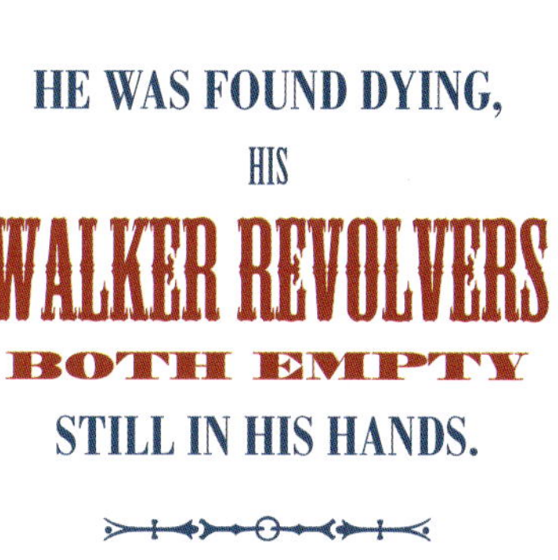

Over the next several years, Colt refined the Walker Model and made it a little smaller, renaming it as the Dragoon Model. The name derived from its supposed use, by mounted infantry who would dismount prior to engaging the enemy. The Dragoon Model, based on the strong points of the Walker, became Colt's first commercial success. Combined with the similar Model 1851 Navy, the diminutive Baby Dragoon and Model 1849 Pocket Revolver, Colt manufactured almost 630,000 firearms of these models introduced within four years of the Walker's production. This period of success was a far cry from the period before the Walker's production. Colt himself credited the Walker with saving the future of his firearms company by giving it the economic boost it needed to survive and succeed.

As for the Walker, it is estimated that fewer than 150 of the original 1000 Walkers destined for the Texas military are still in existence. Seen as the ultimate goal for a serious collector of Colt revolvers, the small number remaining in circulation is a mark of both its usefulness and its weaknesses. Those that did not fail eventually would have been used until they simply fell apart. Most of those still around, such as the example shown in this section, marked "D Company, No. 66", show the wear and tear of 150 years.

THE STANDARD REINVENTED

THE US MODEL 1842

It can be said that one constant of the American West was change. Another was the presence of the military. As the West was settled prior to the Civil War, the territories, from the gold fields of California to the wheat fields of Kansas, experienced both. The population movement required the presence of soldiers along the various routes of travel throughout the West. Soldiers were also a necessity in the settled regions as protection against the dangers that resulted from

US Model 1842 Musket

choosing to build a town in the middle of land that properly belonged to Native Americans. The soldiers of the region needed the most updated firearm technology. Later these "high tech" arms received a second life in the hands of the settlers themselves.

One key firearm in the history of the United States in the West was the US Model 1842 Musket. Although a smoothbore, its percussion action set it apart as one of the first arms of this type adopted by the military. While the percussion ignition system was developed during the first decade of the 1800s, most militaries around the world kept the flintlock in service until the 1840s. The percussion action, regardless of any benefits, was simply too new to be accepted and produced quickly on a large scale by the military establishment. It took fifteen years after the adoption of a percussion action firearm before the Springfield Armory built the last flintlock musket. Even after the adoption of a percussion firearm in 1833, production of these arms barely went above a few thousand until 1844. This level of percussion production was one-tenth the level of flintlock production over this period.

Regardless of the numbers, the percussion or flintlock arms made prior to 1844 were built, effectively, one-by-one. The individual parts were relatively rough when cast and not necessarily identical to other objects of the same type. Each part required additional milling, filing, or other modifications in order to assemble the arms. As a result, the final fit on particular guns was amazingly precise. However, the individual components of these guns were different enough that they would work badly on another arm, if at all.

The effective end of the flintlock period was the same year that the Army finally began the manufacture of an arm that was built from parts that were completely interchangeable. While the parts of arms built at the armories at Springfield, Massachusetts, and Harpers Ferry, Virginia, could often be exchanged with those from other arms made at the same armory, it could not be guaranteed that they would work with parts from the other armory. After the

United States began to manufacture the Model 1842 in 1844, this problem was resolved once and for all. That year,1844, was also the final year of manufacture for the Model 1816 Musket, previously the standard arm for the Army. At 28 years, the 1816 was one of the few arms to surpass a quarter century in American service. It was also in the period of 1844-45 that, for the first time, percussion arms overtook flintlock in numbers produced. If not for a French artillery captain, the Model 1842 would have likely seen a similar record. And the history of the West would have likely been different.

In the late 1840s, Captain Claude Minié developed a bullet for easy and effective use in rifled barrels. Whereas round lead balls were the rule previously, Minié used a heavier conical bullet with a hollowed cavity in its base. The bullet was slightly smaller than the barrel caliber when cast, allowing it to be literally dropped down the barrel. The advantage of this was that the rifle could be loaded much quicker than with a round ball that, with a patch, was slightly larger than the barrel diameter. Upon firing, the skirt-like base of the bullet expanded, engaging the barrel rifling. This greatly improved the effective range and accuracy over similar smoothbore arms.

FOR THE TRAVELER TO THE WEST WHO HAD LIMITED FUNDS, LIMITED SPACE, AND A NEED FOR A CAPABLE ARM, THE SURPLUS MODEL 1842 WAS THE RIGHT WEAPON.

Minié's development sounded the death knell for all military smoothbore arms—including the Model 1842. With an easy and fast method for loading rifles, the world's armies shortly switched over to rifles, sending the smoothbore to the same refuse heap as the flintlock. The American Army developed a percussion rifle, the Model 1855, shortly after this change and ordered an end to the production of the Model 1842. But during its tenure as the Army's long arm, it was an effective arm. As an example, the 1842 saw use in the 1847 war with Mexico, a war that ended with the United States adding almost a third to its area.

With the change to the Model 1855, the Army began to sell the Model 1842s that were not modified to rifled barrels—not even one year's worth of production were modified in this manner—to private individuals and corporations. These individuals and corporations, in turn, sold the guns to other militaries and to civilians. These resellers, predecessors of today's army surplus stores, often modified these arms by cutting the barrel down from the 42" length to a more manageable length of three feet or less. In this format, the modified gun found new life in the hands of many settlers.

Priced at $2 to $5 dollars, the surplussed Model 1842 was much cheaper than the $20 or more asked for many of the hand-built or factory manufactured firearms that normally were for sale in Cincinnati, St. Louis, or other jump-off points for travel to the West. For practicality, the traveler often needed to be able to hunt a variety of game, as he would often encounter deer, pigeon, and animals of all sizes in between. The .69 caliber smoothbore barrel was a true multi-purpose tool. The barrel, approximately halfway between 12 and 16 gauge, could be loaded with a large round ball, buckshot, or birdshot in order to hunt any type of game.

Additionally, this would prevent any need for the settler to carry two or more firearms and the ammunition for each. Supplies for the Model 1842 included commonly available items—percussion caps, black powder, lead ingots, and bullet molds. In the period after the Civil War, this was even more relevant as more arms began to use self-contained cartridges in a dizzying variety of sizes and types. For the traveler to the West who had limited funds, limited space, and a need for a capable arm, the surplus Model 1842 was the right weapon.

While much has been made of the Colt and the Winchester in the annals of Western history, many arms have been overlooked—the Smith & Wesson #3, the Trapdoor Springfield, and the Hawken Rifle, to name a few. However, discussions of even these guns often overshadow the importance of the Model 1842 in the settling of the West. Soldiers and civilians alike used this work of industrial art, whether at the order of the government or in the attempt to find a new life in the distant lands of the country's territories. The technological advancements represented by it showed the future potential American arms. The result of change, it was the victim of change. However, its resurrection as a civilian arm led to its importance in the history of the West.

SAM COLT'S OTHER REVOLVER

THE REVOLVING LONGARMS

The archetype weapon of the Wild West was the revolver. Normally believed by most interested parties to be the Colt Single Action Army, the truth is that there were many revolvers of a variety of types used throughout the history of the West. Pepperboxes, cap and ball revolvers, cartridge revolvers, small guns and large guns, pistols, rifles, and shotguns were made in America and Europe for civilian and military use in urban and rural settings. Across the country agents, stores, and catalogs sold hundreds of varieties, most based on only a few patents. The least common revolving arms were longarms—shotguns and rifles. These longarms had every possibility of being the select longarms of the Wild West, time and technology put an end to this opportunity.

Although many novices to the subject believe that Samuel Colt was responsible for the design, Colt was not the only player in the game. At the time he produced his first arms in the late-1830s, there were several designers in competition, if not well ahead of Colt's production attempts. During the following two decades, a number of developments and problems eventually drove the revolving longarm to the wayside while allowing the revolving pistol to flourish. Colt's stranglehold on his patent, some issues of safety, and high cost were just a few obstacles. Eventually, though, the nail in the proverbial coffin was the introduction of other breech-loading actions—specifically the lever-action repeater.

Colt's first production revolver, not the handgun one would suppose, was an eight-shot rifle chambered for calibers ranging from .34 to .44. While the first models of his production used a ring mounted in front of the trigger to cock the action, Colt's later longarms and all of his handguns were of a different design, utilizing a now-common hammer to perform this task. Of all of the arms manufactured by Colt during his residence in Paterson, New Jersey, the most successful model was the carbine of 1839. This is the arm that Samuel Walker encountered while fighting in the Florida Everglades. If Colt had not gone into bankruptcy in 1842, he may have been able to support himself with this arm alone.

With Colt's bankruptcy and relocation to Connecticut, he would have been out of the gun business for good had it not been for Sam Walker and Sam Colt cooperating with each other. The resulting government contracts for a variety of revolving handguns gave Colt the financial backing necessary for a new start. From 1847 until Colt's death in 1862, the company operated successfully, supported by the various descendents of the Colt Walker, and relying for much of this time on the strength of the patent on his revolver design to prevent competition. The one major design exception resulted in the various models of 1855.

Similar designs for a pocket revolver, a carbine, a sporting rifle, a military rifle, and a shotgun went into production. Derived from the same basic premise, Sam Colt diverged from his

Colt Model 1855 Revolving Shotgun

previous design in a number of ways. A solid frame greatly strengthened the revolver, allowing it to use larger loads of black powder and giving Colt the option to apply the design to long arms. Though this also prevented the owner from easily removing the cylinder, the handgun was very popular, with 40,000 manufactured over a fifteen-year period.

The longarms of this type were very popular during the Civil War, being used by a number of both Union and Confederate units, the latter leading some researchers to falsely accuse Colt of supporting the South. In civilian hands, the success was not as widespread. One of the possible reasons for this is that percussion revolvers could explode if not loaded or maintained correctly. The flame from the chamber being fired could ignite neighboring chambers. On the rare occasions on which this occurred, the shooter would be lucky if the cylinder held together—albeit spraying lead fragments to the front of the gun. It was not unknown for the person pulling the trigger to loose a hand, despite Sam Colt's own instruction to never place your hand in front of the cylinder. This "flash-around" became a folklore-ish element of the history of Colt, but was only part of the problem with the success of these arms.

In 1860 the New Haven Arms company introduced their Henry Rifle to the market. This fast shooting, easy-to-use rifle was a vast improvement over the various revolving designs of the period. Not only was it safer, but it also carried more ammunition and did not take as long to reload. The ammunition was self-contained, allowing the arm to work in rainy weather—something the percussion revolvers of the period could not do. Although the next generation of revolving arms, especially those of Colt, would make use of self-contained cartridges, it would not be until the 1870s that this would occur. Smith & Wesson held the patent that allowed revolving arms to fire metallic cartridges. As with Colt's earlier patent preventing others from developing efficient revolvers, he was prevented from improving on his own design due to the same reason.

WHILE GENERALLY HIGH QUALITY FIREARMS, THE REVOLVING LONGARMS OF THE MID-1800S WERE THE RIGHT PRODUCT IN THE WRONG TIME.

The final cause of the revolving longarm's demise was the cost. The design, development, and production of any of the various revolving designs meant that the individual price of the arms was prohibitive. Colts and other revolving longarms would cost twice as much as quality single-shot arms that could be purchased for anywhere from $5 to $15 dollars. While this was not a problem for the wealthy, the gun manufacturers relied on a large number of purchases among the middle and lower classes. Although Colt seemed to have a reprieve by selling a small number of the Model 1855 arms to the military, the numbers were not enough, especially in light of the need to change the design to accept metallic cartridges.

While generally of a high quality, the revolving longarms of the mid-1800s were the right product in the wrong time. Development twenty years earlier may have led this type of arm to be the "Gun That Won the West." However, Colt's longarms, at one time destined for greatness, simply were too much—too expensive, too cumbersome, and too late in showing up. The issues that were detrimental to the longarms were the strengths in the handguns. Although they may not have been the "Gun That Tamed the West," as their salesmen made them out to be, the Colt handguns were important in the history of the West. And after Colt's initial failure in New Jersey, they were saved as a result of the work done on the longarms in the 1830s and the 1850s.

THE SOUTH'S SHOTGUN

THE LEMAT REVOLVER AND CARBINE

One of the largest movements of Americans took place in the years following the American Civil War. Whether a Northerner or a Southerner, the opportunities available in the wilderness beyond the Mississippi River were great. The presence of gold and silver was well known and cattle operations were still being set up from Texas to Montana. For many, however, the draw was simply the allure of a different life when there was little chance for opportunity in the devestated landscape around them. This allure helped many former soldiers of the Confederate States of America make their decision to press West.

When these former "Johnny Rebs" went west, some took with them a piece of arms history later ignored by all but those interested in the arms of Civil War and the Old West. This history was the product of François Alexandre LeMat, a French émigré to the United States in the

LeMat Carbine

1840s. LeMat practiced as a physician in New Orleans but he also dabbled in mechanical design, specifically where firearms were concerned. In the 1850s LeMat contracted to begin construction of a handgun that added a twist to a standard design.

LeMat's design was based on the standard revolver layout—a revolving cylinder rotating on a center pin. The difference was his replacement of the center pin with a separate smooth-bore barrel for shot or a large bullet. The main barrel was generally bored for a .42 caliber ball

LeMat Revolver

or conical bullet. One of the advantages in using this gun was the extra three shots allowed by the larger cylinder, enabling the user to shoot longer without reloading. The other advantage, and the more famous of the two, was the center-mounted barrel. At approximately 16 gauge, the center barrel of the LeMat was a daunting weapon to face. With a load of shot, the short barrel was effective in close range combat or in a foraging capacity. Paired with the revolver shown is a rarity, a LeMat Carbine. Basically a LeMat pistol with a longer barrel, the carbine was never made in any large numbers.

Besides living in one of the important cities of the Confederate States of America and being a supporter of the rebellion, LeMat was also the cousin-in-law of General P.G.T. Beauregard, one of the more famous cavalry generals of the war. With these allegiances it was only a matter of time before he received a contract for his revolver. The contracted manufacture of the LeMat took place in France and, to a limited extent, in England. While this revolver was purchased by the

AFTER THE WAR MANY OF THE DISPLACED VETERANS OF BOTH SIDES OF **THE WAR BETWEEN THE STATES** WENT **WEST** SEEKING A BETTER LIFE.

CSA for their cavalry officers, only about 1500 of the total 3000 produced were purchased by the CSA for service in the Civil War. Among the users of LeMat's revolver were J.E.B. Stuart and LeMat's aforementioned relative, General Beauregard.

After the war, many of the displaced veterans of both sides of the War Between the States went west seeking a better life. Most of these soldiers carried their military arms with them, whether as a badge of service or to produce in observers the supposition that "This person is carrying a gun so he must know how to use it." Regardless of the reason, the fact that guns were widespread in the West is exactly that, a fact. What is little discussed is that the presence of these guns is a direct result of the strange ending to the most fractious period of the history of the United States. If the conclusion of the war ended as with most other attempted revolutions–with the disarming of the population of the loser by the victor–guns would still have existed in the West, but in much smaller numbers.

LeMat Carbine

Over the last several decades, the LeMat has attained a level of fame that neither reflects its capabilities nor its historical importance. One source of this attention was the 1959 television series *Johnny Ringo*, starring Don Durant. While much has been made of the abilities of the small shotgun built into this revolver, its use required the manipulation of the hammer in order to strike the correct percussion cap. This manipulation is not easy to do safely with a loaded revolver under calm conditions such as those encountered while target shooting. In combat, and while wearing gloves, it would almost be impossible to quickly change the hammer in order to use the center barrel.

Regardless of the issues with the physical manipulation, the LeMat came to represent a number of things—the success of an immigrant, the needs of the Confederate States of America to supply arms to her troops, and the effects of war on a society.

TWO NAVIES FOR THE ARMY

THE COLT 1851 AND 1861 NAVY REVOLVERS

Watch enough realistic movies of the "Old West" and you will notice something—the Winchester rifles and the cartridge revolvers will be missing. "The gun that won the West" and "the pistol that tamed the West" may have been effective marketing slogans, but the truth of the matter is that the various cap-and-ball revolvers were the guns that the people of the West often purchased for serious firepower. Chief among these guns were the various Colt models based on the Dragoon design of the late-1840s. Specifically, the two "Navy" revolvers—the Models of 1851 and 1861—saw much use. Between the two models, Colt manufactured almost 300,000 over a combined period of thirty-four years. Ease of use, reliability, and ready availability of replacement parts and accessories made these guns valued arms in the West. Use of these guns by soldiers and Western figures alike also aided the popularity of these revolvers.

After the success of the .44 caliber Dragoon and its variants, particularly the .31 caliber Model 1849 Pocket Pistol, Colt designed a model that followed the design, but filled the niche between the two ends of the caliber spectrum. At .36 caliber, the 1851 Colt was a revolver that was handy to use, lighter than the Dragoon, and powerful enough to be useful in combat.

Colt Navy Revolvers, Models of 1851 (bottom) and 1861, with detachable stocks

Colt Model 1851 Navy Revolver with detachable stock

It became the first successful "holster" pistol in use in the West. This is an important designation with early revolvers. The earliest handguns, flint or percussion, were large, heavy, and clumsy. This better suited them for carriage in small scabbards mounted to the saddle, leading to the name "horse pistol." The smaller handguns of the period, designed to be concealable and carried in pockets, purses, and the like received the appellation of "pocket pistols." With these designations the use and style of carry of a particular gun was apparent.

Possibly the most confusing point about the purpose of this revolver was that it was not intended for use by a particular navy. The term "Navy" has more to do with the roll-stamped battle scene on the cylinder than anything else. Featuring a face-off between the Mexican and Texan Navies, this image is often missing on these guns as a result of years of use by the owner. This fact alone should be enough to prove the popularity and longevity of these guns. Wear from holster leather and normal handling is not normally considered rough, yet the stamped metal was worn smooth on these guns. This gun and the Colt Model 1861 Navy, a streamlined version of the 1851, were both produced until 1873 when Colt finally began production on the Single Action Army, the gun most people associate with the company. Additionally, there were versions of each designed to accept a small, detachable stock, effectively allowing them to be used as carbines.

Both the 1851 and the 1861 were popular guns that became a large part of Colt's income stream throughout the twilight years of percussion firearms and the American Civil War. One of the more famous owners of the Colt Model 1851 was James "Wild Bill" Hickok. Carrying a pair of 1851s tucked into his belt butt-forward, Hickok was a true character of the West. After drifting around the West as a hired gun for several years, he became the Sheriff of Hays County and, later, Abilene, Kansas. It was during this period Hickok received the Navy revolvers he is best known for. In the 1870s, Hickok worked for William F. "Buffalo Bill" Cody as part of Buffalo Bill's Wild West. Hickok's last days were spent in Deadwood in the Dakota Territory. It was here that he died in 1876, still carrying his Navies three years after Colt stopped manufacturing them in order to focus on the Single Action Army. Shot in the back while playing poker, Hickok never had a chance to get off a shot. As a result of the condition of Hickok's finances, his prized Navies were sold off to pay for the funeral.

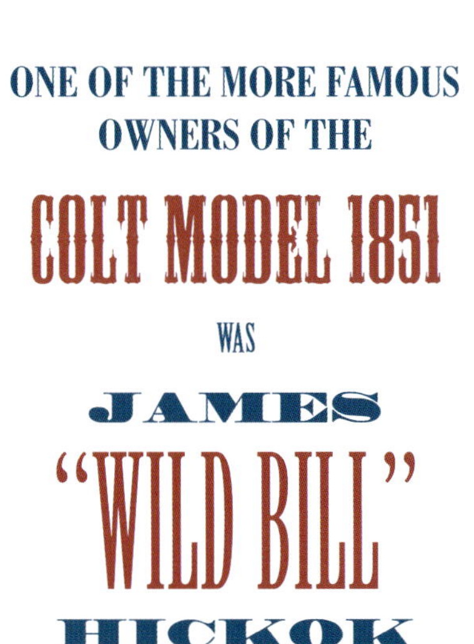

In addition to the likes of Hickok, the Navy was popular on both sides of the Mason-Dixon Line during the War Between the States. Although the larger Model 1860 Army revolver was the primary sidearm for the Union Army, many soldiers carried Navies of both vintages. Also, companies other than Colt often made these revolvers. A number of small companies in the North, South, and even Europe manufactured thousands of unlicensed copies of the 1851 and the 1861 during the Civil War. Carried predominantly by infantry soldiers who did not want to carry the larger 1860 Army, the Navies saw much in the way of combat and acquitted themselves in all areas of the war.

The effect of the Navy on the future of firearms development was such that many manufacturers continued to make cartridge firearms in mid-sized calibers such as .38 Colt, .38-40, and .41 Colt. The name "Navy" continued to be used into the 1890s on arms that were designed for the civilian market as well as the United States Navy. Today the .38 Special and a variety of 9mm cartridges fit the same niche as mid-power handgun cartridges. The all-around effectiveness of these guns of the West helped make them as popular as they were. The sturdiness and longevity helped them stay popular after the widespread introduction of the cartridge arms by the major gun companies. Although they were not the most high-tech guns in the West, they were two of the most efficient and best-respected guns of the period.

JAMES B. "WILD BILL" HICKOK WITH HIS MODEL 1851 COLT NAVY REVOLVERS

PART
III

"CIVILIZING"
THE
WEST

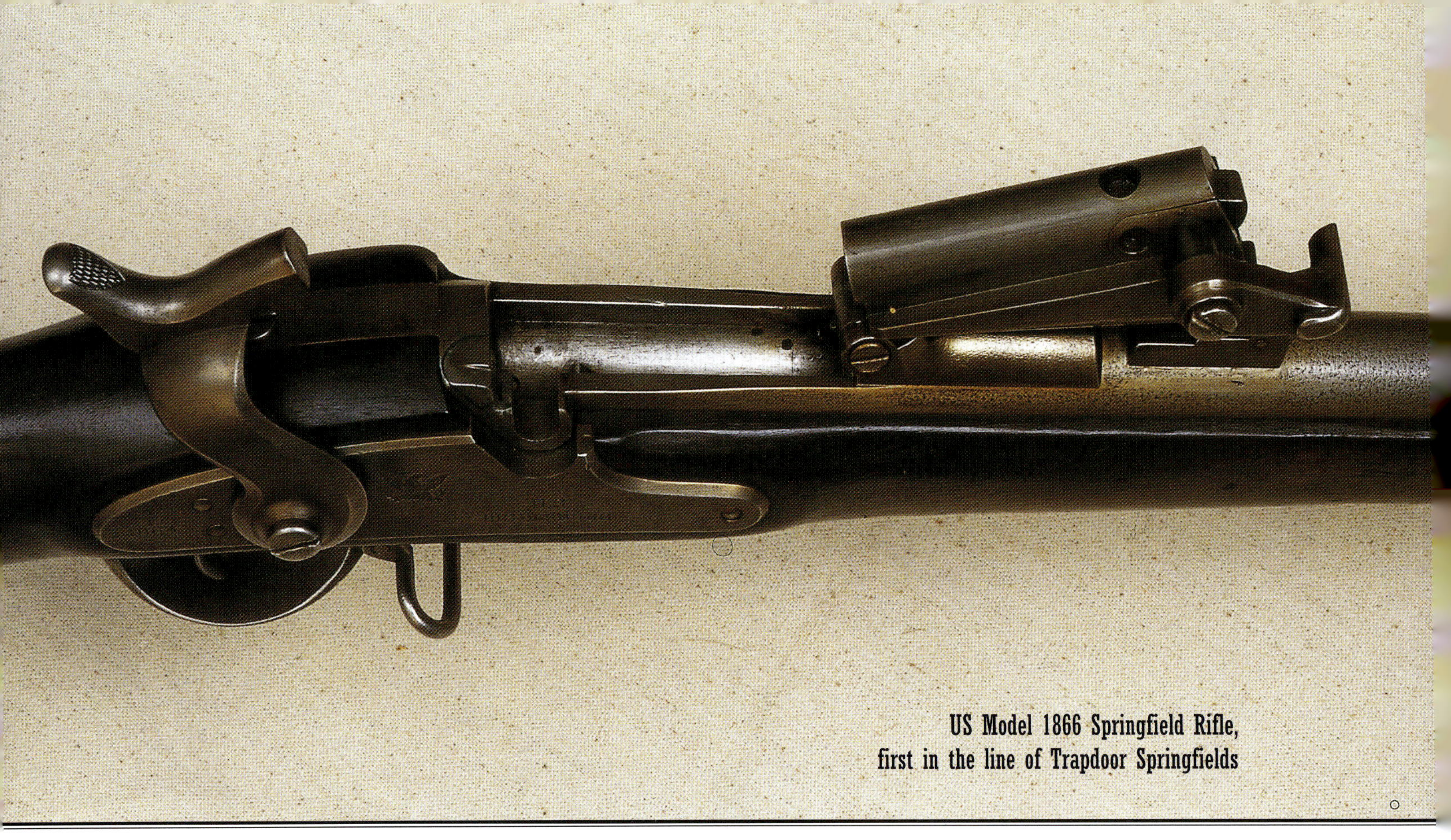
US Model 1866 Springfield Rifle, first in the line of Trapdoor Springfields

THE NEW STANDARD

THE "TRAPDOOR" SPRINGFIELD RIFLE

Recently much has been made of the longevity of the M-16—the standard rifle of the US military from the 1960s into the 21st century. The M-16 has joined a small fraternity of long-lived military arms that survived in service for over a quarter century. The list of these arms for the United States is very short, due primarily to the many technological advances that have taken place during the country's short existence. While famous firearms of the past have been successful, technology would soon cast them aside for an improved replacement.

Flintlocks beget percussion guns; smoothbores beget rifles; muzzleloaders using loose powder and ball beget breechloading cartridge guns; and so on. The few rifles that stayed in place for over 25 years were the M-16, the Model 1903, and the Trapdoor Springfield. It was changing technology that led to these rifles coming into use, as well as their eventual replacement. Oddly, while change led to the adoption of these arms, it was a combination of resistance to technological change, and political wrangling, that led to them staying in use.

The American Civil War created an odd mix of hesitation and excitement regarding martial technology. The old guard within the Army's Ordnance Department, typified most famously by Brigadier General James W. "Old Fogey" Ripley, Chief of Ordnance during much of the Civil War, resisted any activity requiring change, whether this included the use of metallic cartridge ammunition or repeating arms. Eventually, President Lincoln had Ripley retired for this mindset.

The younger and lower ranked officers in the Ordnance Department saw the benefit of these new advances, appreciated the caution with which they should proceed.

A number of well-made firearms were available in the civilian market, using a variety of repeating or single-shot actions and a variety of ammunition. These arms, used to some success during the Civil War, were quite popular in many circles. However, the Union Army, in choosing a new firearm also understood the necessity to dispose of hundreds of thousands of rifled muskets in the transition to the new model. The wise designers attempted to modify the rifled musket currently in use by the Army rather than replace it with a new design.

Although a variety of designs were forwarded, the proposal made by Erskine Allin was the one chosen by the Army. Allin's design was the simplest and least expensive of those proposed. It consisted of milling out a section of the breech and attaching a hinged door to the top of the barrel. This design allowed a metallic cartridge to be fired, satisfying the younger, forward-thinking officers. However, it was incapable of repeating fire, satisfying the old guard. Much of the success behind this design came from Allin's familiarity with the military arms procurement system, a result of many years working at the Springfield Armory as the master armorer.

The two versions of the Allin Conversion of the US Army Rifle eventually became the US Model 1865 and then Model 1866 Rifle, little more than continuations of the conversion program. This firearm, also available as a carbine, was produced in .50-70 caliber. The variation standardized in 1873 was chambered for the smaller .45-70 with .45-55 for the carbine. The success of this rifle was well known. As with the Winchester Model 1873, the US Model 1873 was popularized by a film, this one starring Gary Cooper and titled "Springfield Rifle." While being interesting as an introduction to a great firearm, including some close-up footage of the operation of the rifle, there are some problems. As with many Hollywood interpretations of the Old West, there are issues of authenticity. Cowboys are seen carrying Colt Single Action Army revolvers and the soldiers are seen with the 1873 Model of the Trapdoor. Unfortunately, the film takes place during the Civil War, predating both arms by almost a decade.

A factual story regarding the Trapdoor and its importance took place in the Wyoming Territory in the late 1860's. On December 21, 1865, eighty-one cavalrymen were killed protecting a woodcutting expedition. While many people have accused Captain William Fetterman as the major force behind the massacre named after him, fingers should instead point

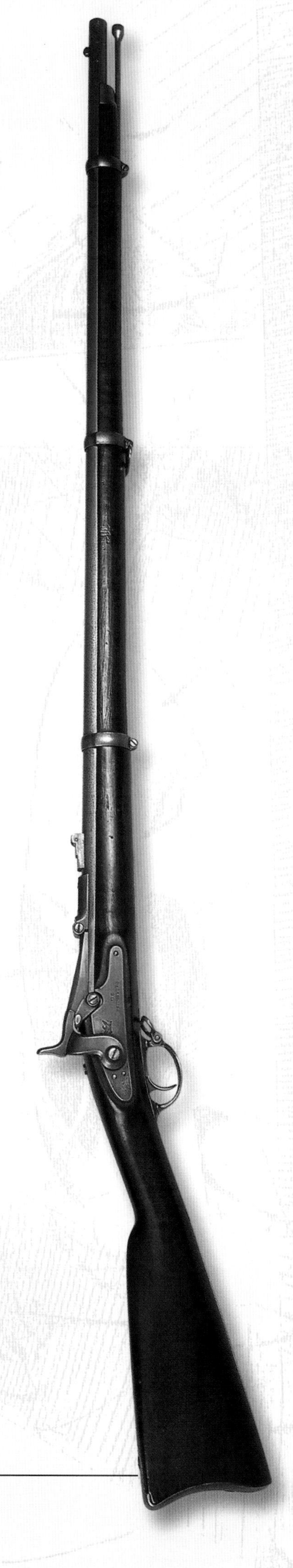

US Model 1866 Springfield Rifle, first in the line of Trapdoor Springfields

to the arm used by the military at the time—the old muzzle-loading Springfield musket that was the standard Union arm in the recent Civil War. The shortcomings of this rifle, namely the slow reloading time and the necessity to stand up and stand still when loading, in order to do so quickly and correctly, allowed an enemy to draw a volley of fire, and then charge while the firing unit reloaded. This allowed Fetterman's unit to be overrun in short order.

The Wagon Box Fight was an example of how the new breech-loading rifle changed the face of battle in the West. On the August 2, 1867, a woodcutting party left Fort Phil Kearny. Twenty-six soldiers and four civilians were attacked by a war party led by Red Cloud. The work detail circled their wagons and flipped over the wagon boxes to form an impromptu fortification. The Indians sent a small raiding group in to attack. This raid was turned back under a volley of fire. A larger group of Indians then charged, expecting the soldiers to be busy reloading. Little did they know that the US Army had just switched over to the new cartridge-firing breechloaders. The soldiers, aided by the civilians armed with repeating rifles, were able to keep up a constant barrage, at times having poor shots reload for those who were sharpshooters. The thirty soldiers and civilians held out for over three hours before reinforcements showed up and the Indians left the battlefield.

THE 30 SOLDIERS AND CIVILIANS HELD OUT FOR OVER THREE HOURS BEFORE REINFORCEMENTS SHOWED UP AND THE INDIANS LEFT THE BATTLEFIELD.

The only supposed blemish on the Trapdoor's record was the Battle of the Little Bighorn in 1876. While this battle turned out poorly for Custer, the primary issue was one of numbers, not technology. Taking fewer than 500 soldiers against an army of thousands was the real cause behind the demise of the 7th Cavalry. As for the armaments used, researchers have determined that only 30-50% of the Indians were armed with firearms. Additionally, approximately 80 different types of firearms have been found to have been used at the battle, with few of these being repeaters. Based on the research, most of the Indians faced that day were armed only with either bows and arrows or muzzle-loading trade guns.

Regardless of any shortcomings in design—or in the military procurement system—the Trapdoor Springfield had what it took to survive in the West. It was only when other technologies surpassed it to the point that the Trapdoor was obsolete that the US government chose another rifle. The Trapdoor then continued in the service of various state militia organizations in the Spanish-American War and even on the home front in very limited numbers during World War I. This rifle and all of its variations was one of the tools that allowed the United States to expand in the manner it did after the Civil War. The effectiveness can be seen in, if nothing else, the longevity of its service to the country.

FROM CIVIL WAR TO PLAINS WAR

INDIAN-MODIFIED SHARPS CARBINE

Before the American Revolution, the colonial economy was limited in development because of the Crown's policies regarding manufacturing in the American Colonies. There were restrictions placed on many goods that were derived from raw materials harvested in the colonies. Although craftsmen were capable of creating these goods, the government prevented them from taking the middleman—the British manufacturer—out of the picture. The later economy of the West was very similar to a colonial system of rule. The major difference is that the urban West was, in many cases, not able to support manufacturing facilities capable of producing many of the finished products in the West. These products, ranging from stagecoaches to

Sharps Model 1859 Carbine, Indian Modified

six-shooters, were simply too complex for the typical Westerner to manufacture. As a result, Westerners were often employed in an industry that involved the harvesting of raw materials or the support of this activity. The money earned from this employment allowed the citizens of the West to purchase the products created with the fruits of their work.

In the period before the American Civil War, the settlers who moved west supplied themselves with the best arms available. Besides the many muzzleloaders available, there were also newer revolving arms from Colt and others. In the 1850s a new single shot, breech-loading arm became the most popular firearm of this type until metallic cartridges became widespread after the Civil War. This firearm, the Sharps Percussion Carbine, was lightweight, accurate, and easy to load. During the much of the Civil War, the Sharps was one of the more common arms in use by the Union forces. It was such a well-respected firearm that the Confederacy set up a factory that produced about 5,000 knockoff copies of the Sharps.

The utility of the Sharps made it popular in the West, especially in places like "Bleeding Kansas"—the territory that came to be a flashpoint in the confrontation between the nation's abolitionists and pro-slavery forces. Henry Ward Beecher, an abolitionist preacher in Brooklyn, New York, raised money to purchase illicit arms for shipment to Western anti-slavery forces led by John Brown. Simply shipping these arms to the West became an adventure as the federal government outlawed the arming of these groups. In response, the various factions shipped the guns to the West in crates marked "bibles." This story led to the generic naming of these Model 1853 Sharps as "Beecher's Bibles," though they were not the only Sharps to arrive in the West.

With the initiation of hostilities beginning the Civil War, the Hartford, Connecticut, Sharps factory quickly increased production. During the course of the war, more than 100,000 percussion Sharps were manufactured for the Army. With the South's capitulation, the need for these arms disappeared, relegating the vast majority of them to the secondary market as military surplus. Being greatly marked down in relation to the newer cartridge arms made by Sharps, the price of the percussion guns allowed many Americans to obtain them. The citizens who migrated to the West carried these guns and others with them as they traveled to mining, lumber, and ranching areas.

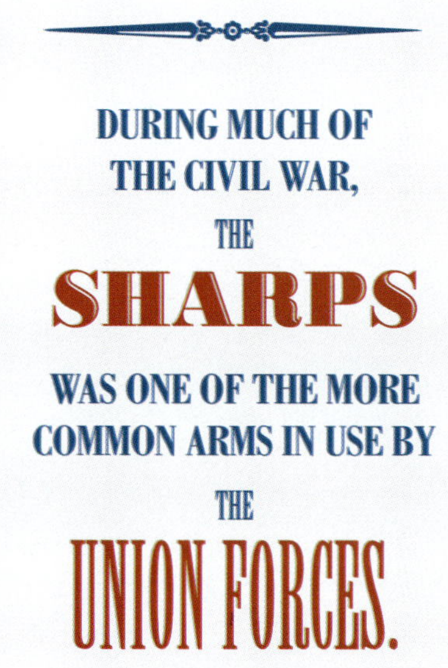

The exploitation of the West's resources by the white settlers supplied the East with the materials needed for manufacturing. A specific example of this relationship involved the hides of cattle and buffalo. The hunting of buffalo benefited a number of industries, including fashion, railroads, and manufacturing. While the effect on clothes and food, for fashion and railroads, are simple to understand, manufacturing involved the use of the animal's hide to create machine belts for use in the factories of the day. The need for these belts in locations like Hartford, Connecticut—home for both Colt and Sharps, among others—created a sellers market when it came to the hides. This situation led to the mass slaughter of Bison by hide hunters normally armed with Sharps rifles.

In the expansion of this industry, there were conflicts between the newcomers and the Native Americans already residing in the American West. While some of these conflicts ended peacefully, many resulted in violence. In these cases the victor was able to take anything left by the loser. This was perhaps the most common way in which Indians obtained modern firearms. As alternatives, a secondary market opened up when many Civil War era rifles and carbines were sold to surplus companies. Regardless of any regulations, many of these guns ended up in the hands of Indians and others.

Any firearm in Indian use received harsh treatment. At home there were no gun racks or other ways to easily take care of or protect guns. With no holsters or scabbards to speak of, much less a saddle designed for such use, these guns received little or no protection while traveling. Commonly seen on these guns was a large amount of saddle wear on the wood parts. Indians would often carry their arms by hand, allowing them to rest across their laps while riding. The constant handling received by these guns caused them to wear prematurely, fall apart, or become damaged beyond repair. Many guns from the period show signs of repair in the form of wire or rawhide wrapped around the muzzle or stock in order to hold the gun together.

Besides any materials used to stabilize the gun's condition, many Native Americans decorated their firearms by tying feathers and shells to the frame, marking parts of the wood, and hammering brass tacks into the stock. These tacks have become an issue in modern gun collecting. A number of otherwise plain firearms have been modified over the past century with the addition of brass tacks in order to increase the value as an "Indian Gun." The Sharps Carbine seen here, however, is the real McCoy, with a tack design created by an unknown Native American.

The chain of production in the firearms industry was a "chicken and the egg" affair. Some of the materials necessary for production came from the West, as did the money required for Westerners to purchase these guns. The guns, themselves, helped many of the Westerners earn their livings as buffalo hunters, ranchers, or gun dealers. The Native Americans, on the other hand, rarely had opportunities to purchase these arms. The irony is that many of the arms they obtained were like the one seen here, responsible for the much of the annihilation of the bison, the animal on which their lifestyle and livelihood depended.

SPORT AND WAR

GEORGE CUSTER REMINGTON ROLLING-BLOCK

June 25th, 1876, was a typical hot, dusty day in the rolling hills of Southeast Montana Territory. Typical, that is, with the exception of the column of United States Cavalry preparing to attack a village of 8,000 to 10,000 Sioux and Cheyenne. The outcome of the battle and the long-term effects of this attack on national policy have been well discussed elsewhere. The commander of the Cavalry, one George Armstrong Custer, has also been the topic of countless articles, essays, and biographies.

There is a cottage industry that has grown up around the history and mythology concerning the events of this day. The discussions surrounding Custer's personality, ability as a leader, and especially his decision to forego the use of his Gatling Guns can start up conversations similar to those of 125 years ago. Those conversations, marring the jubilance of the nation's centennial celebration of the Declaration of Independence, were full of conjecture regarding how the

Indian defenders could annihilate a large part of Custer's command.

Regardless of the various causes and outcomes of the Battle of the Little Big Horn, the discussions eventually return to the person of George Custer. He has been seen as a hero, a fearless soldier, a tactical genius, a great leader, and a dangerous adversary. He has also been described as a braggart, foolhardy, a strategic buffoon, overly proud, and flamboyant. Regardless of these apparently contradicting views of Custer, he can in some ways be seen as a typical officer of the Plains War Army.

As a graduate of West Point, and last in his class at that, Custer went into the US Army as an officer. During the American Civil War, Custer was brevetted (given a temporary, nominal promotion) from the rank of Lieutenant Colonel to Brigadier General. After the war, Custer continued his service as in the western United States. With the rank of Lieutenant Colonel, Custer commanded a regiment of cavalry—655 horsemen and supporting soldiers. He and his officers would have been seen as minor royalty and potentates by some in the West. Others would see certain officers as despots or worse.

Regardless, the social status of the military officer in West did offset the negative side effects—few or no promotions, dreadful duty stations, an enlisted corps of uneducated soldiers, and, the classic observation, months and years of stultifying boredom separated by moments of sheer terror. The officer corps was allowed to bypass some regulations occasionally. They could wear non-traditional uniforms, carry non-standard firearms, take short "hunting trips" while in garrison or on the march, and sidestep a variety of ethical checks that are currently in place in the military of the 21st century.

Among Custer's non-standard firearms were his Webley Royal Irish Constabulary revolvers (covered elsewhere in this work) and a pair of Remington rolling block hunting rifles. When in the field with his regiment, Custer often took one of the rifles, leaving the other at home. This was not uncommon as many officers had a "special" rifle that would be carried for the sole purpose of recreational hunting. Captain Gustavus Doane, who later was an early explorer of the region of Yellowstone National Park, often left the column for days at a time to hunt while the 2nd Cavalry Regiment traveled from Wyoming to Montana. It is believed that he had a special, non-standard rifle of his own.

CUSTER AND HIS OFFICERS WOULD HAVE BEEN SEEN AS **MINOR ROYALTY** AND **POTENTATES** BY SOME IN THE WEST.

The Remington rolling block was a good choice as the personal rifle of an Army officer. Truly one of the early great hunting rifles of the cartridge era, the Remington was known as having one of the strongest actions of that period. Although greatly overshadowed by the Sharps Rifle in use by buffalo hunters, both big-game hunters and long-range shooting competitors used the rolling block.

Possibly the most famous use of the rolling block in competition was at the 1874 Creedmoor Competition at the Creedmoor Range on Long Island, New York. The American team, using rifles manufactured by Remington and Sharps, won the competition against the Irish team armed with Rigby rifles. Firing at targets at ranges of 800, 900, and 1000 yards, the American team scored 934 to the Irish team's 931 (out of a possible score of 1000). Surprising the Europeans, the American team took the trophy. The long history of Americans using rifles is seen by some as a cause of this victory.

The demise of Custer is well known. The status of the guns carried by him into battle is unknown. One of two rolling blocks owned by Custer is intact. Given by his widow, Elizabeth,

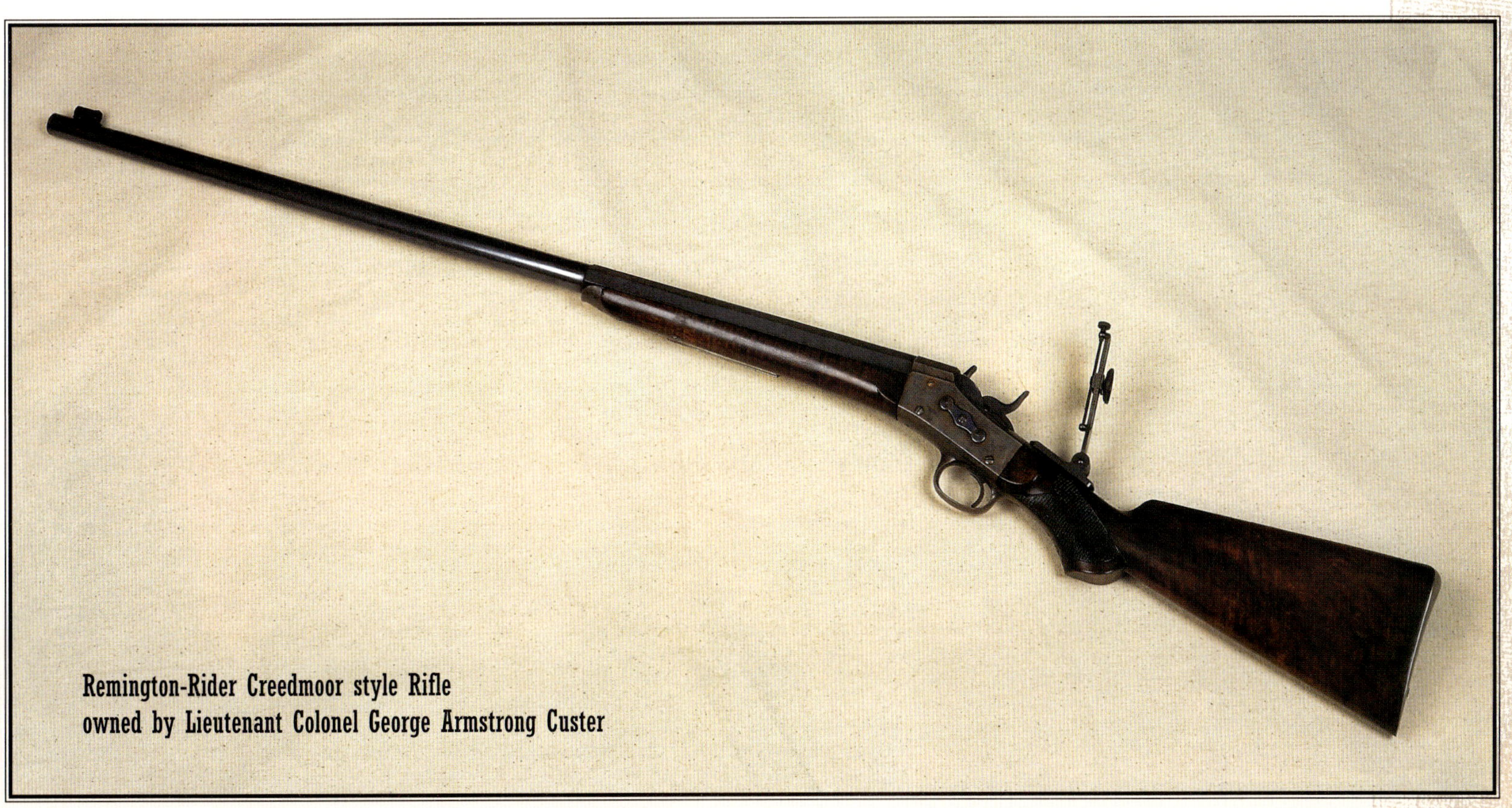

Remington-Rider Creedmoor style Rifle
owned by Lieutenant Colonel George Armstrong Custer

to the Winchester Repeating Arms Company in 1883, this rolling block is still available for viewing at the Buffalo Bill Historical Center, in Cody, Wyoming. And while Custer has been a lightning rod both for the renewal of energy in the conquest and pacification of the West and also for the expansion of American Indian rights, this gun represents much more than one man or one event. It represents a specific type of rifle and even a social class of the American West.

EUROPEAN GUNS, AMERICAN BATTLES

WEBLEY REVOLVERS

In many studies of the history of the West, the Colt Model 1873 revolver is key in discussions of firearms. However, there were many firearms being used in the Wild West other than the guns of Samuel Colt. While some of these guns were made in the United States many guns were made in Europe or elsewhere. The market for these guns was a result of the expense of American firearms and the need for firearms manufactured under a different design philosophy. While many of the handguns and long arms manufactured in America were designed for use in rural or frontier areas, the firearms developed in Europe were often designed for and used by citizens of urban areas. Regardless, these firearms were widely accepted in the Wild West.

One company that manufactured such firearms was Webley of England. For many years Webley had manufactured firearms for the British military. These arms were generally large caliber revolvers that were quite dependable and sturdy. The first Webley pistol used by the British was the Royal Irish Constabulary Model of 1872, a .45 caliber double-action revolver that served well in the British colonies around the world and later in World War I. Webley also made guns for use by private citizens of England. One such gun was the Bulldog, a civilian version of the New Model Royal Irish Constabulary revolver of 1883. This revolver was chambered for .455 caliber. While not quite in the class of the .44-40 and .45 Colt, it was a good large bore pistol cartridge in comparison to many of the cartridges used in the West.

One advantage of the Webley revolvers was their stout compactness. While being robust firearms that could fire large caliber ammunition, the civilian handguns were actually quite small when seen in relation to similar guns. This may have been the reason why one of the West's most famous, or infamous, characters normally armed himself with two Webley 1872 RIC revolvers. The man in question was George Armstrong Custer, the commander of the Seventh US Cavalry Regiment.

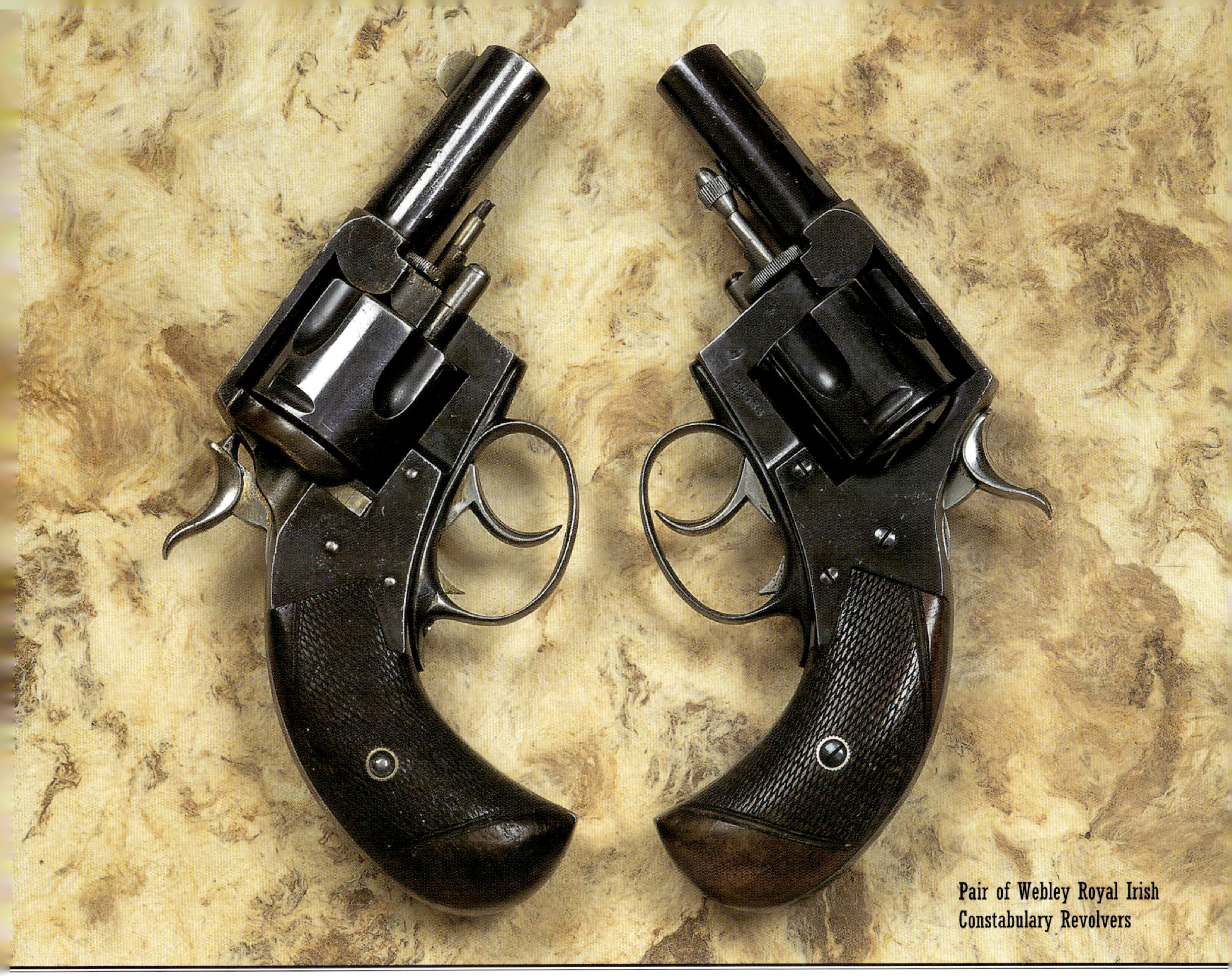

Pair of Webley Royal Irish Constabulary Revolvers

During the period in which the Battle of the Little Big Horn took place, different units of the frontier army used the Colt Model 1873 Single Action Army, the Smith & Wesson Schofield, or the Remington Model 1875 Single Action Army. As discussed in the previous section, officers, however, could use any sidearm they chose. Custer's choice, the Webley, had several advantages over the other arms. While the service revolvers were all single-action, the Bulldog was a double-action, allowing the user to fire as quickly as he or she could pull the trigger. The small size of the Webley and the ability to fire it without the need to cock the hammer prior to each shot meant that it was easier to handle in combat.

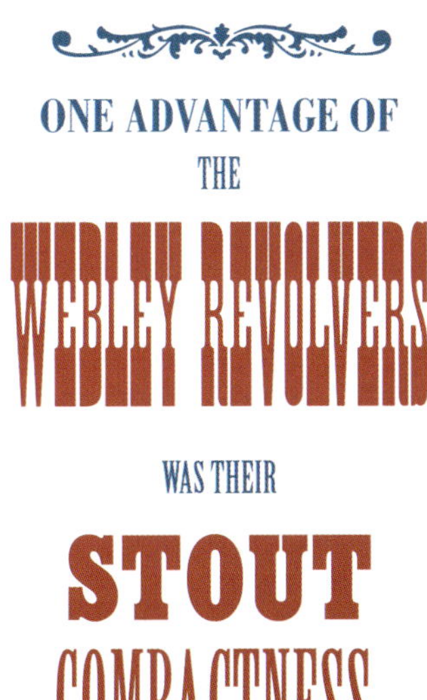

The downsides to using this non-standard weapon ranged from durability to supply. The inner workings of the early double-action revolvers were often very intricate and easily damaged. The ammunition was only a civilian purchase and not available through the normal military supply chains. Thus, when the owner's supply of ammunition ran out or if the mechanism failed while on the frontier,

ONE ADVANTAGE OF THE WEBLEY REVOLVERS WAS THEIR STOUT COMPACTNESS.

the RIC (and its ammunition) became only so much dead weight. The ammunition became an additional issue with the Webley as it could only be loaded with five rounds. Lastly, the short barrel (2.5" to 4.5", depending on the model) reduced accuracy and velocity in comparison to the service weapons.

Regardless of any apparent strengths or weaknesses of the Webley, their use did not help Custer in the hills above the Little Big Horn River—not that this was through any fault of the firearm. The debacle in the Montana Territory did nothing to affect the popularity of the Webley or the other European arms that found their way to the frontier. A number of American firearms dealers, like Benjamin Kittredge of Cincinnati and Schuyler, Hartley, and Graham of New York, continued to import similar arms from England, France, Belgium, and Germany. Whether they were the large-bore guns like the various Webleys or the small-bore copies of the Smith & Wesson Numbers 1, 1 ½, and 2, the European guns were legitimate options in the West.

THE YELLOW BOY

INDIAN-MODIFIED REPEATING CARBINES

A large part of the story of the American West involves the relations between the European settlers and the native peoples who had been living undisturbed for millennia. These relations were affected greatly by the differences in technology. While the technology used by the Europeans in the early 18th century was greatly below today's level of technology, the Indians living on the plains effectively saw it as magic. The use of technology by Native Americans in the eastern region of the United States had several hundred years to grow to relatively the same level of technology. The plains tribes, however, faced a huge paradigmatic shift: going directly from the Stone Age to repeating cartridge firearms in the space of less than four generations.

This technology shift lead to huge changes in the way of life of the Plains Indians. Firearms allowed them to kill their prey more effectively and efficiently. Although the bow used on the plains was effective up close, the firearm gave the Native American a greater edge and a greater level of safety when hunting. This also translated into changes in how the various tribes related to one another. In the same manner that the European settlers gave firearms to "friendly" tribes, the tribes would jockey for position within the good graces of the "great white father" in the east in order to receive these firearms. While the American government and many settlers simply looked to pacify various tribes, there were tribes that use this as an opportunity to impose their will on other tribes that were not yet armed with the advanced weapons that showed up in the West.

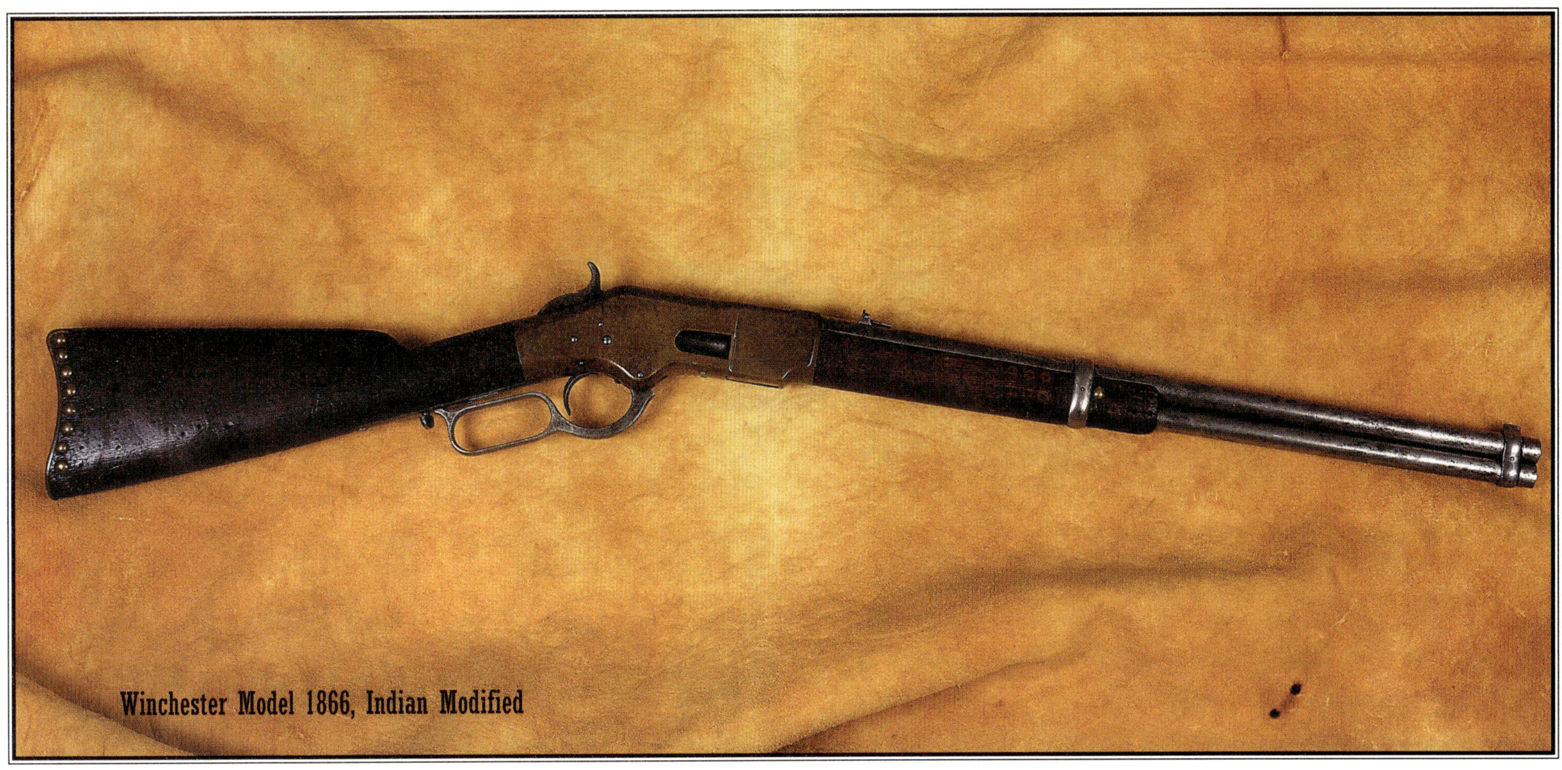
Winchester Model 1866, Indian Modified

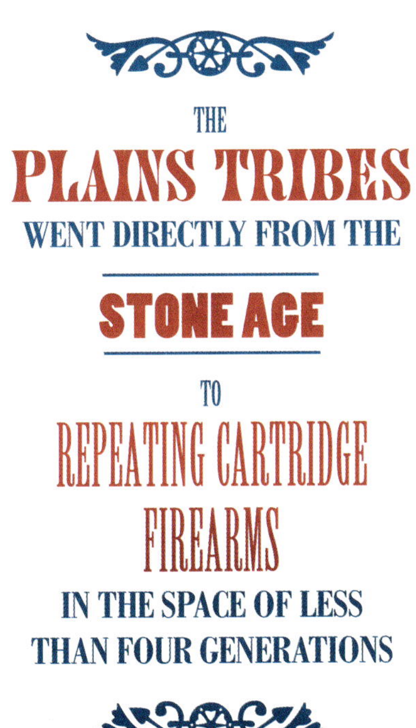

Possibly the most famous of these firearms was the Winchester Model 1866, also known as the "Yellow Boy." The successor to the famed Henry rifle of the Civil War era, the 1866 was the first product of the Winchester Repeating Arms Company. While the intellectual property and patents had already passed through the hands of several companies and individuals—including those of Smith & Wesson—it was a shirt maker who took hold of this company and turned it into one of the few companies that is still manufacturing today.

Although the Henry rifle was a masterpiece of firearms technology for the period, the Model 1866 increased on the performance and durability of this arm by making one small change:the addition of a loading gate on the right side of the frame. This loading gate allowed the user to load single rounds into an enclosed magazine tube, rather than the slotted tube seen on the Henry. An enclosed magazine prevented dirt and other objects from entering the magazine and jamming the action. Additionally, the user no longer had to load the magazine by compressing the magazine spring and rotating the muzzle, an action that could damage the spring if done incorrectly or hastily.

The main attraction to the model 1866 came from the sizable magazine capacity. The '66 could carry thirteen or seventeen rounds of .44 rimfire ammunition, depending on the model. Although the .44 rimfire cartridge was relatively low powered when compared to the .50-70, and later .45-70, cartridge used in the Springfield rifle, the sheer firepower that could be produced by a Model 1866 was much greater than that produced by the single shot Trapdoor. The Wagon Box Fight in the Wyoming Territory in 1867 was a perfect example of this power. A force of twenty-six soldiers and six civilians held off over 800 Indian warriors for several hours—in no small part due to the repeating rifles carried by the civilians.

Among the Indians, this increased firepower led to a similar apparent increase in the power of the warrior who carried such a firearm. The association of a particular warrior with this rifle can often be seen in the decorations and designs affixed to a personal weapon. Many objects could be used to change the appearance of these guns—rawhide strips, tacks, and feathers were quite commonly seen on such firearms. These decorations could tell a story about the owner, his experiences, and the position he held within the tribe.

In the way that the Indians related to their firearms, it is obvious that there was more to their culture than was appreciated at the time. While the European looked at his arms simply as tools for attack or defense, the Indian saw his arms as much more. The arm was a symbol of honor, status, and potential. The better the weapons owned by an Indian, the better the chances for that Indian to succeed in tribal life and in combat. If the Europeans would have understood this, things may have turned out differently in Anglo-Indian relations.

A FORCE OF TWENTY-SIX SOLDIERS AND SIX CIVILIANS HELD OFF OVER 800 INDIAN WARRIORS FOR SEVERAL HOURS—IN NO SMALL PART DUE TO THE REPEATING RIFLES CARRIED BY THE CIVILIANS.

ANNIE OAKLEY POSING
WITH A MARLIN MODEL 1890

PART
IV

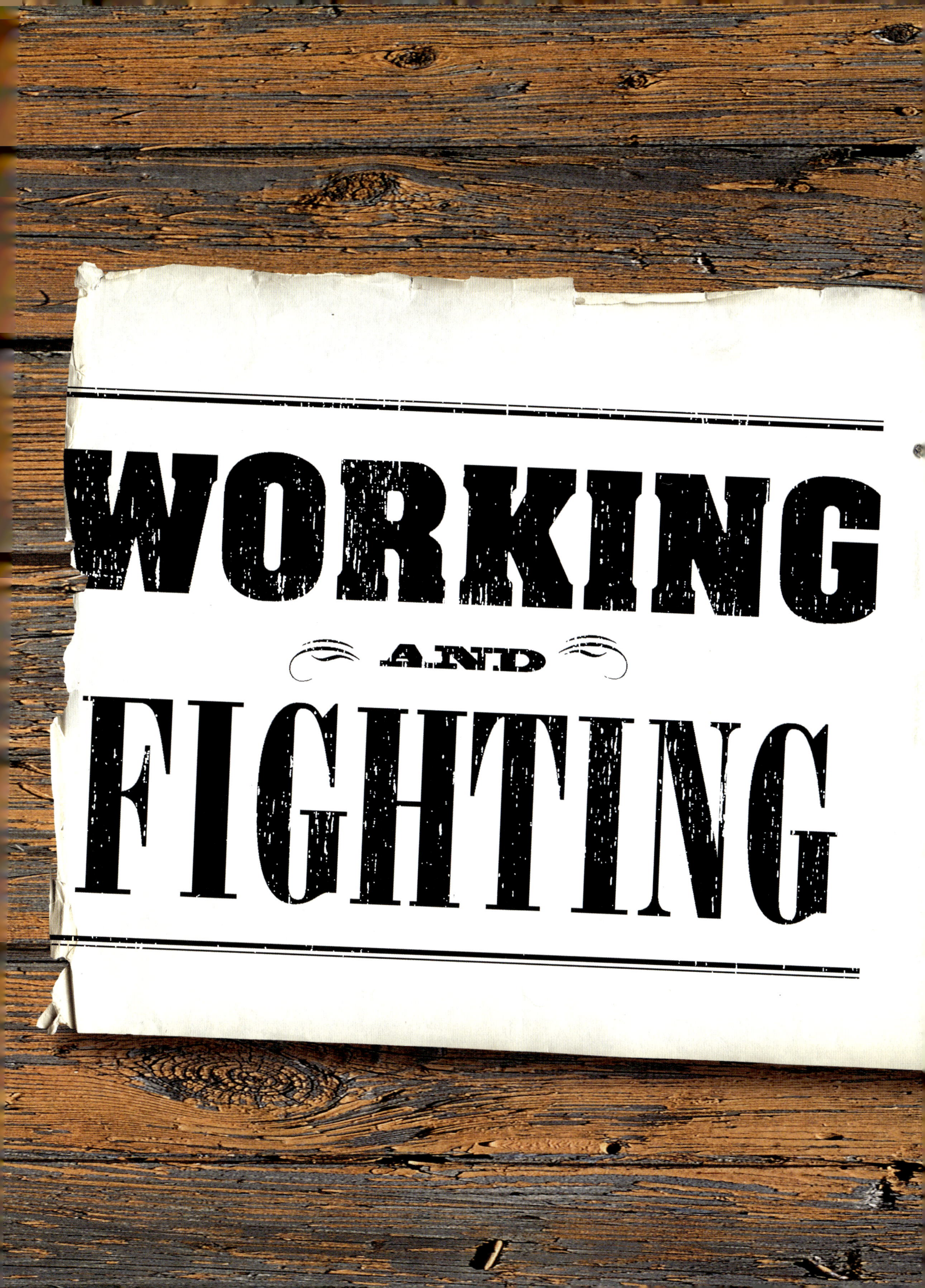
WORKING
AND
FIGHTING

HUNTING FOR HIDES

THE SHARPS BUFFALO RIFLE

Humans and guns has not always been a good combination. In many locations around the world, animals have been brought to extinction or near-extinction through over-hunting. While this over-hunting has affected a number of animals, the best American example of this interaction is the American bison, more commonly known as the buffalo. Once numbering over thirty million and possibly twice that, there was a point in the 19th century at which the bison numbered only about 1,100. Depleted by hunting and the mistaken belief by many that the resources of the West would never run out, the symbol of the American West almost went the way of the Passenger Pigeon and the Dodo bird.

Sharps Model 1869 Carbine, modified by Freund

ONCE NUMBERING

OVER

THIRTY

MILLION

AND POSSIBLY TWICE THAT, THERE WAS A POINT IN THE 19TH CENTURY AT WHICH THE BISON NUMBERED

ONLY

ABOUT 1,100.

Sharps Model 1869 Carbine, modified to fire cartridges

Although bison had once ranged as far east as the Chesapeake Bay, by the time of the early 1800s, the range of the bison was limited to the area between the Rocky Mountains and the Mississippi River, home of the various Plains Indian tribes. Their dependency on the bison meant that they had to follow bison's migration from Mexico to Canada and back. Early European artists like George Catlin and Karl Bodmer captured the importance of the bison in the lives of these tribes, while recording the West in a virtually pristine state. During this period, Catlin observed the earliest influences of the encroachment of European traders on the Plains culture. In the 1830s at Fort Pierre, a fur trading post on the Missouri River, Catlin watched as over 500 Sioux hunters killed 1500 buffalo for their tongues within sight of the trading post. These tongues were shortly traded at the post for a variety of items. According to his journal entry, the majority of the bison corpses were allowed to rot, a preview of the treatment afforded the buffalo hunted by white hunters in the 1870s.

In the 1850s and 1860s, the expansion of the railroads and the growth of mining and logging in the West led to the need for large amounts of food for the work camps. Professional hunters were hired to procure. The most famous of these hunters was a tall scout in his twenties named Bill Cody. In the period before he earned his famous nickname, "Buffalo Bill", he was simply another buffalo hunter tasked with providing food. Working for the Kansas-Pacific

Railroad, Bill's job was to produce the meat from twelve bison a day. He did this for a nine-month period starting in 1867. This total came to over 3,000 bison. While a respectable sum, this was not extraordinary. But when hunting to provide for all of the various camps across the West compounded this damage, the effect can be better understood. By the end of the 1860s ,bison could rarely be found within forty to fifty miles of a railroad track or established town.

The real damage to the bison population occurred during the 1870s. Buffalo hides had become a prized commodity for use as clothing, rugs, and drive belts in factories. The resulting method of obtaining these hides almost finished off the bison for good. Whereas the meat hunters generally rode on horseback and shot individual bison at a run, the hide hunters found a stationary location, or "stand", from which to hunt. This "stand" hunting would allow the hide hunter to kill forty to fifty bison in a one hour period. After the hunter was done, a crew would move in and literally pull the hide from the bison, often removing the tongues as well. As the hunting season often lasted several months—longer in Montana and the Dakotas—hunters could shoot fifty to sixty days of the year. A hunter could have been responsible for over 3,000 bison during a short season, and it was possible for some hunters to double this over the course of the year.

IN THE 1830S AT FORT PIERRE, A FUR TRADING POST ON THE MISSOURI RIVER, CATLIN WATCHED AS OVER 500 SIOUX HUNTERS KILLED 1500 BUFFALO.

The rifle used by the stand hunters would need to fire a large bullet in order to easily and quickly kill the game, be heavy enough to minimize the recoil and be resistant to the heat of repeated firing. It also had to be capable of high accuracy at ranges of over 500 yards, and employ metallic-cased ammunition to make the process of reloading easier. While a number of manufacturers made rifles of this type, the preferred rifles were manufactured by the Sharps Firearm Company of Hartford, and later Bridgeport, Connecticut. Sharps gained its reputation during the American Civil War as the choice of the 1st and 2nd US Sharpshooters. During the widespread hunting of the American bison, many of the buffalo-hunting rifles were purpose-built for this activity; though a large number of these rifles were simply modifications of earlier percussion firearms of Civil War vintage.

Henry Gerdel, a Wyoming buffalo hunter, used the Model 1869 Sharps carbine pictured here. His rifle, originally chambered for .50-70, was re-chambered to accept the larger .50-90 cartridges. The barrel was replaced with a heavier barrel with different sights, both more suited to buffalo hunting. This work was done by the Freund Brothers firm of Cheyenne, Wyoming, the most famous of the frontier gunsmiths who specialized in this work.

Despite the low numbers of the 1800s, there are now about 350,000 bison in the wild and in captive herds. While this number sounds safe, it was only after a century of careful conservation that this number was reached. By the turn of the 20th century, many Americans realized that this animal needed to be preserved in order for it to survive for future generations. It was only through the wise actions of later hunters and others that this survival appears to be ensured.

Smith & Wesson Model 3 Revolver carried by Joseph Wasson while employed by Western Union

A SMITH & WESSON WITH WESTERN UNION

A SMITH & WESSON NUMBER 3

One of many firearms that had to spend time in the shadow of the Colt Model 1873 Single Action Army Revolver was the Smith & Wesson Model 3 Single Action Revolver. Originally designed to accept a number of .44 caliber cartridges, it was carried by the likes of Buffalo Bill, Annie Oakley, and Wyatt Earp. Used frequently on the American frontier, it was also chosen as the service revolver for the Russian Army in the 1870s. The pistols manufactured for the Russian contract in Springfield, Massachusetts, and copies (some licensed, some illicit) manufactured in Berlin, Germany, and Tula, Russia, put the Model 3 over the top when compared with the Colt by numbers alone.

Predating the Colt Single Action Army by three years, the Model 3 was the first handgun manufactured to fire a large, effective cartridge. While being .44 caliber, the list of rounds available for different versions can be dizzying. While most were chambered in .44 S&W (a.k.a. .44 American), some early pistols were chambered for .44 Henry. This was the same cartridge used in the Henry Rifle and the Winchester Model 1866, making this pistol one of the first cartridge pistols to allow interchangeability with a rifle, predating the combination of the matched Colt and Winchester in .44-40 by several years. Another first was the adoption of this pistol by the American military, making it the first cartridge revolver selected for American military use.

In 1873 Smith & Wesson began work on a variant ordered by the Russian government. Visibly different due to a spur extending from the triggerguard, this pistol led to a number of future changes in the firearms industry. The request for a new type of cartridge led to the use of the .44 Russian. This cartridge became the primary large bore cartridge for Smith & Wesson throughout the rest of the century. It was particularly effective as a target round and was quite popular with military, law enforcement, and entertainers. In the 20th century, this cartridge became the basis for the development of the .44 Special (1907) and .44 Magnum (1955) rounds, both helping the success of later Smith & Wesson pistols.

PREDATING THE COLT SINGLE ACTION ARMY BY THREE YEARS, IT WAS THE FIRST HANDGUN MANUFACTURED TO FIRE A LARGE, EFFECTIVE CARTRIDGE.

The next iteration of this design, the Schofield revolver, became one of the more famous pistols of the American West. Faced with competition from Colt for military contracts, Smith & Wesson had to redesign their revolver to make it more attractive to the government. One of these changes was the introduction of another new cartridge, the .45 S&W, effectively a shorter version of the .45 Colt. A variety of mechanical changes aided in meeting the government requirements. By 1877 the Army ordered 8,000 Schofields and 15,000 Colts, showing that the Schofield must have been at least competitive. Besides widespread use in the military, many Schofields were later sold to Bannerman and the firm of Schuyler, Hartley, and Graham for sale in the West, often with the barrel shortened and the pistol nickel-plated. A number of surplus Schofields found their way into the hands of the Wells Fargo Company. These pistols have reached a mythic level of notoriety in the intervening century due to various attempts by forgers to sell non-Wells Fargo revolvers as such.

The later versions of the Model 3 led to an increasingly confusing web of configurations, ammunition and design changes. In addition to new chamberings in .44, Smith & Wesson began to produce revolvers in various .32, .38, .41, and .45 caliber loadings. Revolving rifle versions, with a removable stock, were introduced, though only in small numbers. The final variant of this pistol was a double action revolver, a version that became especially popular as the country moved toward the 20th century.

One example of an early Model 3 revolver, SN 17691, is a pistol carried by Joseph England Wasson, an employee of the Western Union Company. The pistol is chambered for .44 S&W, is nickel-plated, and has the original 8" barrel. Wasson was born in 1813 and died in 1891. It is believed that he purchased this pistol in Missouri (presumably St. Louis) in 1873 or 1874. He spent much of the next decade traveling the West for Western Union before

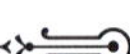

settling in San Francisco. The pistol then remained in his family for four more generations before arriving at the Cody Firearms Museum. This pistol, a type popular with many famous (or infamous) Western personalities, was carried instead by one person who represents the true Westerner; someone who tried to make a living while (knowing or not) he helped to support an important aspect of the American West.

A LITTLE KNOWN SUCCESS

THE EVANS REPEATING RIFLE

Among the many untold stories of the West are those of arms invented by enterprising designers. Although many people are familiar with the names of Winchester, Colt, Smith, Wesson, and others, these companies often benefited from the men they hired more than the man who owned the company, regardless of how successful a businessman he was. For every Winchester, there is a Henry, King, or Browning. Smith and Wesson received their start as the result of work begun by Hunt and Jennings. While Sam Colt developed his own designs for his firearms, the company also benefited greatly from work by Root, Burgess, Thuer, and Browning. Not all of the firearms companies depended only on the work of others, though. Ball, Bullard, Evans, Spencer, Triplett & Scott, Warner, and others who manufactured repeating rifles during the 1800s produced many firearms based primarily on their own designs.

Evans Sporting Rifle

During the American Civil War the most common arms used by the Union were the various rifle muskets of a generally similar type, the Sharps Carbine, also of a generally similar type, and the rifles and carbines produced by the Spencer Repeating Rifle Company. These three arms each represent a different style of arm. The various muzzle-loading arms were the last hurrah of the previous five centuries of military history. About to be eclipsed by the use of breech-loading cartridge arms, the cap-and-ball muzzleloader was of the highest quality available for such a weapon. The Sharps Carbine, the most popular and common cavalry arm of the early war, was the next step in the progression of technology. Still utilizing the percussion action of the muzzleloader, the Sharps was a breechloader, allowing the shooter to reload from horseback or the prone position. Although not yet capable of utilizing a metallic cartridge, the Sharps would truly come into its own as a hunting rifle on the plains of the West.

The third of this group of firearms were the arms of Christopher Spencer. Basing much of his design on the successes of the earlier Sharps, Spencer created the first truly successful repeater used by the military. This arm, equipped with a seven-shot tubular magazine in the stock, enjoyed much popularity due to the sheer volume of fire available. With the additional use of metallic cartridges and a specialized loading tube, the Spencer became the most popular cavalry arm of the war, overtaking the Sharps by the end of the war. This popularity served the Spencer well after the Confederate surrender at Appomattox as it became the common repeater in military use in the American West. Unfortunately for the company, the government eventually decided to surplus the Spencer in favor of the Trapdoor Springfield Carbine as a cost-cutting measure. Although the Springfield was a single shot firearm, the size and range of its cartridge was better suited for the open areas of the West.

THE SHARPS CARBINE, THE MOST POPULAR AND COMMON CAVALRY ARM OF THE EARLY WAR, WAS THE NEXT STEP IN THE PROGRESSION OF TECHNOLOGY.

With the forgoing of the modern technology by the military, the few companies who supplied the Union Army quickly went out of business, as there were no contracts available to support them. Partially as a result of better technology and partially as a result of better designs, new repeating arms did appear on the market in the decades following the Civil War. Winchester continued to improve on the design of the Henry Rifle. Eli Whitney, Jr. saw to the expansion of his company's product line with the addition of a variety of breechloading arms of both single shot and repeating designs. The Evans Repeating Rifle Company of Maine entered the fray with an untried repeater that saw a measure of success, as it became the most popular non-Winchester repeater of the 1870s.

With a total production of less than 13,000 from 1873 to 1879, the Evans guns were not in a position to threaten Winchester's stranglehold on the repeating arms market—Winchester having produced over 180,000 repeating arms during the period of the 1870s. However, Winchester was relatively traditional in its designs, leading to few major changes over a forty-year period. Evans, on the other hand, gained attention through the odd design of the magazine. While tubular, like the Spencer, the magazine was a helical design. Resembling a corkscrew, the magazine design forced the cartridges in a circular motion from the rear to the front of the stock, eventually ending in the chamber. The cartridge, a

.44 caliber centerfire, came in two lengths, short and long. The difference between these cartridges and the guns for which they were designed meant that the Evans could hold a staggering 28 or 34 cartridges. A few early production models could hold 38 rounds. Not until the introduction of the Thompson submachine gun would an American gun again hold that much firepower.

Although the Evans was only produced for less than a decade, it was an important arm. The cartridge was comparable to the .44-40 used in the Winchester rifles of the same period. Despite an increase in weight, the Evans could hold more than twice the ammunition of the Winchester or any other shoulder arm of the 19th century. Unfortunately for Evans, the company simply did not have the name recognition of the larger Winchester. With the entry of Colt and Marlin into the repeating arms trade, Evans, Whitney, and Bullard—the three largest makers of repeating arms after Colt, Marlin, and Winchester—could not compete. Although they made fine guns, the larger companies could do it cheaper, while receiving more press. These corporations were able to capitalize on the work of skilled employees while focusing on the bottom line. Many of the smaller companies simply could not keep up as the designers and the business managers were often the same people. As a result, these little-known actors in the story of West still have problems being heard.

Belgian Double-Barrel Shotgun, marked "Adams Express Company"

RIDING SHOTGUN

THE COACHGUN

A common fixture of Western films is the stagecoach. New characters show up on the stage. Ne'er-do-wells are sent packing on the stage. Bandits rob it and the law sends out a posse to recover the strong box. The hero can save the heroine as the runaway stage coach heads toward a ravine. Besides the use as a plot device, the main characters can share a ride, building a relationship that is of later use. These uses of the coach as a prop are an indication of the importance of the stagecoach in the history and storytelling of the West.

From the earliest days of the European colonization of America, coaches for hired transportation and mail service were a common sight. For those who could afford the services, the coach offered travel to the next village, town, or city, with these different legs called "stages." These inter-city coaches were the fastest means to transfer news and information. From New Hampshire to Georgia, the colonies shared news and ideas in the decades leading up to the American Revolution. These ideas and the movement that evolved from them eventually led to the open revolt that took place against England.

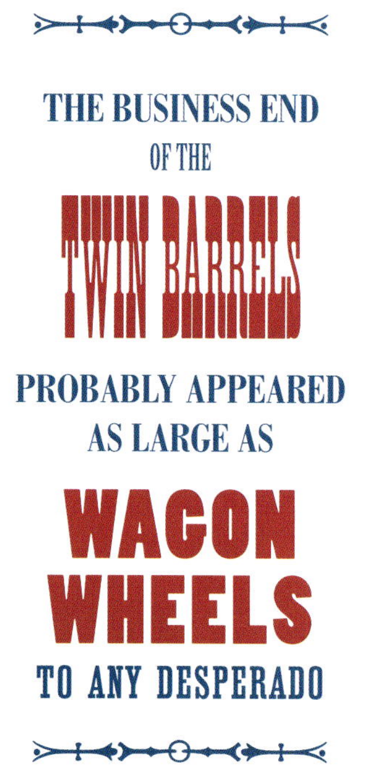

A few decades later the stage continued to hold its importance. As the Frontier passed the Allegheny Mountains and moved to the Mississippi, the coaches followed once roads were established. While the coaches fought with riverboats for long-distance commerce and passengers on the Ohio and Mississippi Rivers, they held on by supporting the areas between the rivers and the distant towns and cities. This service—between rivers and population centers in the hinterlands—became a permanent fixture of the West as the front lines of settlement passed the Mississippi River.

The gold fields of California saw the stagecoach provide service to another region of the country in the same manner as it did in the colonies. With small towns popping up amidst the older, established Spanish communities, goods and travelers needed a means of transport, and money was necessary in order to pay miners for any gold ore found. The transport of money and gold in coaches led to the eventual occurrence of holdups.

Holdups, unfortunately, were not a new development. Stage holdups and "highwaymen" were a relatively common occurrence in Europe and, to a lesser extent, in New England. However, the highwayman of the 1850s had access to a new tool—the revolving handgun. Previously the highest level of technology that was available to the criminal was a side-by-side shotgun or other multi-barrel arm. The other option was to carry a variety of firearms in order to fire multiple times without the need to reload. Those on the stage often carried guns as well, whether they were the driver or a passenger, but that armament would normally only be enough to prevent a robbery by someone armed with something less than a firearm.

With the use of revolvers and other repeating arms, it became necessary for the driver and his assistant to up the ante, so to speak, and be better prepared to protect their passengers and increasingly valuable cargo. It is a result of this escalation that riding in the front passenger seat of an automobile is called "riding shotgun." Invariably, the rider in this position on the stage was a company employee or guard holding a shotgun. This guard was primarily in place to protect the strongbox and any other cargo on the coach, if not the passengers.

The importance of the strongbox is what has led many people to believe that Wells, Fargo & Company ran stage lines across the West. On the contrary, nothing could be further from the truth. While many of the strongboxes in use were owned by Wells, Fargo, there were many different coach lines in many parts of the West, with each line running a number of routes, depending on the coaches they owned and the manpower (and horsepower) at their disposal.

Wells Fargo actually did run a series of routes in the West, but this only existed for a three-year period. The largest coach line of the period was the Butterfield Overland Stage Company. Lasting only a few years before the Civil War, Butterfield made its name contracting with the government to carry mail to California and back

The "Coach Gun" in this section is a 12-gauge side-by-side, or "double barrel", shotgun manufactured in Belgium. The barrels have been cut back to 20" to aid in maneuverability. The short barrels also increased the spread of the buckshot or birdshot, improving its use as a defensive weapon when fired from the moving coach at distances of 20 yards or more. At close range, the business end of the twin barrels probably appeared as large as wagon wheels to any desperado who happened to be trying to get rich the hard way.

As with the arms owned by ranches, mining companies, and other concerns, the various coach lines purchased guns for the use of the guards on any coaches. The Adams Express Company, original owner of this shotgun, started as one of the most successful express companies in New England. With the 1849 Gold Rush, they became the first express company to service California. The company operated in California until 1855. In the same manner as the ranches, the coach lines stamped or branded their company name into their guns. It is in this area that the fame of the Wells, Fargo name has been greatly overused. Many shotguns of the 1800s have been fraudulently marked as property of Wells, Fargo & Company, greatly (and unethically) increasing the value.

As time went on, the weapons technology improved to the point that lever-action and slide-action shotguns began to replace the older double barrel shotguns. These new shotguns gave everyone involved more firepower, as did the widespread use of repeating rifles and carbines. This period lasted for only a short time, however, as roads and automobiles soon replaced the stage in the West. As with other changes, the memories of the West soon became all that existed except for the few coaches that remained as museum relics and movie props. Elements of this period live on in our slang, commercials for a national bank, and our imaginations. As with other aspects of Western History, much can be discovered simply by examining our own culture.

TWO GUNS AND TWO GUNMEN

COLT LIGHTNINGS AND THUNDERERS

Talk to anyone involved in law enforcement and ask him or her about their worst fears. High on their list will be the worry of being outgunned by a criminal. As a result of the supposedly new theme of criminals being armed with more deadly weapons, many law officers are being armed with more powerful firearms than were in use only a few years ago. This process is not new.

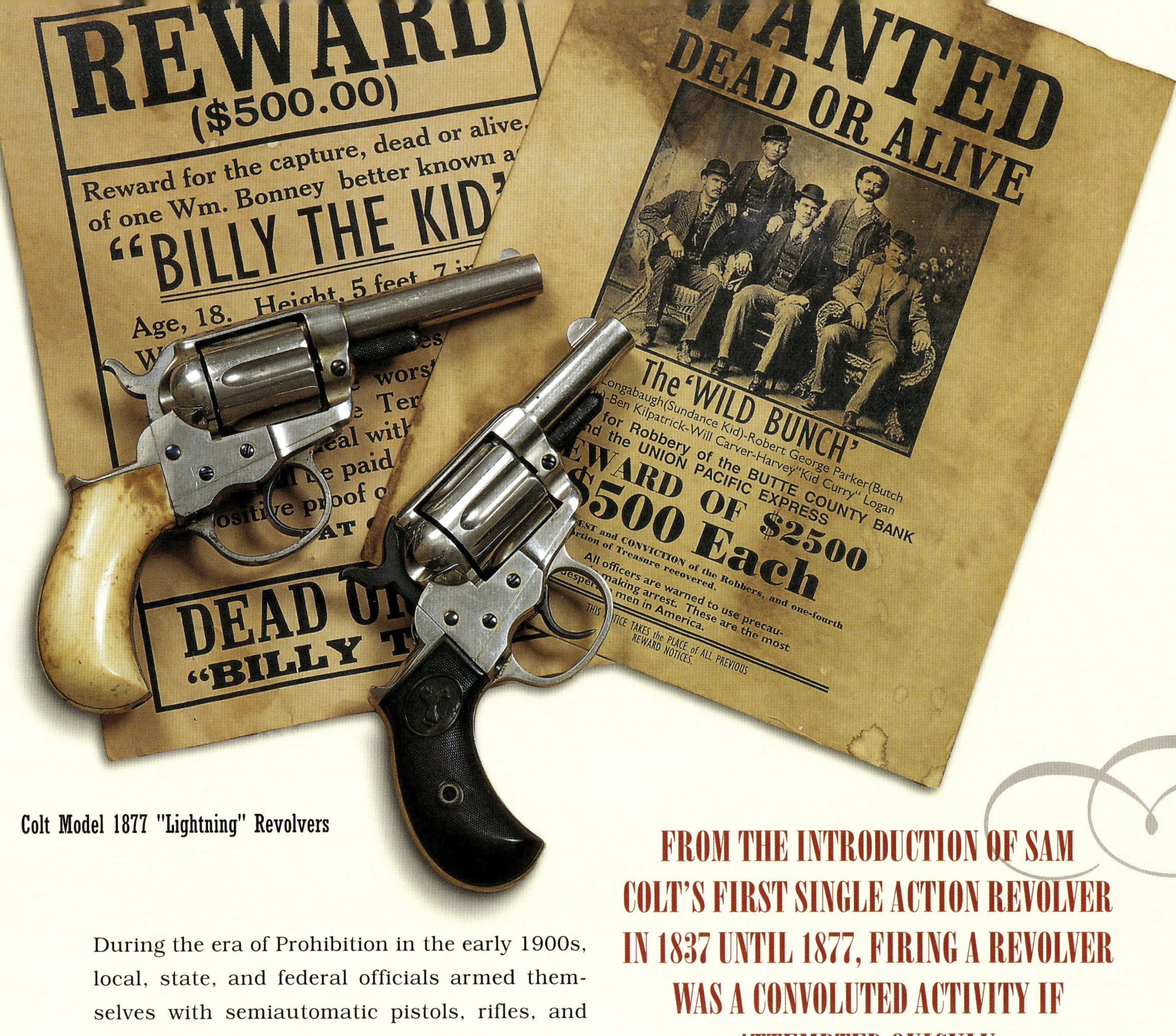

Colt Model 1877 "Lightning" Revolvers

FROM THE INTRODUCTION OF SAM COLT'S FIRST SINGLE ACTION REVOLVER IN 1837 UNTIL 1877, FIRING A REVOLVER WAS A CONVOLUTED ACTIVITY IF ATTEMPTED QUICKLY.

During the era of Prohibition in the early 1900s, local, state, and federal officials armed themselves with semiautomatic pistols, rifles, and shotguns as well as Tommy guns and Browning Automatic Rifles in order to level the playing field between them and the well-armed criminals they faced. Even farther back in time, the criminals and lawmen of the late 1800s faced a similar arms race as technology gave them the ability to fire faster and faster. Other than the obvious introduction of repeating rifles and shotguns, the introduction of double action revolvers not only allowed the gunman to fire faster, not being required to thumb the hammer, but also to fire two-handed, with a revolver in each hand.

From the introduction of Sam Colt's first single action revolver in 1837 until 1877, firing a revolver was a convoluted activity if attempted quickly. This was the result of how a single action revolver worked. As the trigger only performed the "single action" of releasing the hammer, causing the revolver to fire, the shooter was required to manually cock the gun's hammer, setting the action. If the person firing the gun was shooting at stationary targets, this was not a problem. However, if the shooting was done quickly—or if someone else was shooting back—the thumbing of the hammer with the shooting hand or the Hollywood-invented "fanning" of the hammer could easily lead to fumbling and inaccuracy. While there were a few shootists who armed themselves with a pair of single action revolvers–"Wild Bill" Hickok and his twin Colt 1851 Navies come to mind–these specialists were few and far between.

Colt 1877 "Lightning" Revolver

This changed when Colt introduced their first double action revolver, the Model 1877. Allowing the shooter to both cock the gun and release the hammer with a single trigger pull, this revolver allowed the shooter to perform two actions. The person firing the gun could empty the revolver as fast as they could pull the trigger. This would speed up the first shot out of the holster. It also freed up the non-firing hand for any number of activities, from handling the reins of a horse to using a second revolver. Both of these benefits increased the short-term firepower available to the gunslinger. These new guns also allowed the amateur gunfighter to break into the shooting world as the guns were more user-friendly, to use a modern term. Within a few years of the Model 1877's introduction, Colt added another double action model and Smith & Wesson introduced several of their own as smaller manufacturers began to copy the guns of the larger companies.

Colt's Model 1877 was manufactured in only two chamberings, .38 and .41 Colt. As a result of advertising by the Cincinnati gun distributor Benjamin Kittredge, these two guns received the nicknames "Lightning" and "Thunderer," respectively. Kittredge, also responsible for the "Frontier" nickname given to Colt's Model 1878 Double Action Revolver, was one of the largest distributors of firearms to the West. These were successful guns, over 100,000 were built and sold in the first twenty years of its production—a number slightly lower than the number of Colt Single Action Armies produced during the same period. Two famous personalities who chose the Models of 1877 and 1878 as their preferred arm were William "Billy the Kid" Bonney, Jr., and John Wesley Hardin.

Colt 1877 "Lightning" Revolver

Both of these gunslingers were involved in events that took place in the Southwest. Although Hardin was older than Bonney was, he outlived him by many years. Bonney's exploits, covered in a number of films and books, both fiction and non-fiction, are well known to many people who have only a cursory knowledge of the period. From his beginnings as a petty criminal to his involvement in the Lincoln County Range War, much has been told, but no small amount of it is pure fiction. However it is known that he often carried a Model 1878. Dead in 1881 at the age of twenty-one, Billy left a legacy of violent history that was intense for the period, if only as a result of the short timespan of his activities

Hardin, a Texas native, started on his violent career as a teenager, similar to Bonney. Although he is probably less well known than Bonney, he is considered by many historians as probably the deadliest gunfighter in the history of the West. It is possible that this is what led to a prison term for the murder of a sheriff's deputy, allowing him to live instead of ending his life in an ambush. Pardoned in 1892, after serving fifteen years of his sentence, Hardin eventually moved to El Paso. Little did he know that he would be dead within a year of his arrival in West Texas. During the last few years

Billy the Kid with a Winchester Model 1973 and Colt Revolver

TWO FAMOUS PERSONALITIES WHO CHOSE THE **MODELS 1877 & 1878** AS THEIR PREFERRED ARMS WERE **WILLIAM "BILLY THE KID" BONNEY, JR.,** AND **JOHN WESLEY HARDIN.**

of his life, Hardin owned at least three Model 1877 revolvers of both calibers. One of these revolvers was used famously by Hardin to shoot playing cards in the street at the grand opening of a bar in which Hardin was a partner. In 1895, Hardin met his end at the age of 42, twice that of Bonney. Call it coincidence, but both of these gunfighters known for using double action revolvers were killed with Colt Single Action Revolvers.

While these two gunmen were known as skilled shooters, the guns they carried may have been the additional tool that separated them from the run-of-the-mill criminals who existed throughout the West. This new technology aided many double action shooters, as they were able to keep up with more skilled single action shooters. This extra touch undoubtedly changed the result of more than one mismatched face-off in a bar or dark alley. This technological advantage led to others picking up these guns in an attempt to even the odds. This arms race has continued to the modern world as newer technologies continually face off against each other in the hands of today's gunslingers.

THE ECONOMICS OF RANCHING

THE REMINGTON ROLLING-BLOCK

One of the common scenes of the mythic West, whether in literature or cinema, is the cowboy on horseback. With a pistol on his hip and a carbine in hand (or in a scabbard under his saddle), he was ready for anything. With all of his gear and the ability to use it, the scene was set for an adventure. Although the story could involve fighting any of a dozen sorts of desperado, riding through the night with any sort of precious cargo, or taking the herd from Texas to Montana, his belongings—horse and saddle, pistol and carbine—were ready to face the challenge . . . or were they?

Everything about this description is relatively accurate. Although most days were filled with choking down dust and doing simple, albeit dangerous and important, chores, the cowboy did face some extreme circumstances and activities. He rode a horse and he carried a gun or two.

Ranch-owned Remington Model 1871 Rolling Block Rifle

For many cowboys, the only things he generally owned were the saddle he rode on during the day and the bedroll he slept on at night. As for the other equipment, he often had to use whatever equipment and horse was available through his employer.

Any serious ranch in the West, from the King Ranch in Texas to the Flying D Ranch in Montana, owned a selection of arms of different types—handguns, rifles, and shotguns. These arms comprised a small arsenal from which employees could draw for use in their daily duties. As an example, gun scholar Herb Houze unearthed records of a large operation in the Midwest purchasing 300 firearms, including shotguns, .45 caliber Colt revolvers, Winchester Model 1873 rifles, and other guns. The total bill for these guns would have been more than $8000–a fortune at that time.

FOR MANY COWBOYS, THE ONLY THINGS HE OWNED WERE THE **SADDLE** HE RODE ON DURING THE DAY AND THE **BEDROLL** HE SLEPT ON AT NIGHT.

Nelson Story, the first cattle baron of Montana, provided another example of this type of procurement. In 1866, he went to Texas in order to move 3000 head of cattle to the Gallatin Valley of Montana. Before leaving Texas, he purchased enough Rolling Block Rifles and Colt Navy revolvers to outfit his entire company. The trip to Montana was mostly uneventful until he reached Wyoming. After sneaking his herd and men out of an Army controlled area, he lost two men and a number of cattle to an Indian attack. They retaliated and continued on to Montana. That herd became the basis for the early cattle industry in Montana.

An examination of the economics involved in ranching reveals the determining factor in fire arms acquisition. During the back half of the 19th century, the income for a cowboy ranged from $15 to $40 per month. With this salary range, the guns considered to have won the West were too expensive at about $20 for a new Colt and $40 or more for a new Winchester. In the example above, the large ranch purchase included 100 paired revolver/rifle sets costing at least $60 each. As the price of a new Winchester or Colt represented the salary for one to three months, the cowboy would have to decide how his money would be spent. With the various expenses for food, liquor, and companionship, cowboys may have needed to save up for many months in order to purchase a new firearm. However, there was another option.

With the end of the Civil War in 1865, there were hundreds of thousands of surplus firearms in the military's arsenal. When these arms were sold to civilian dealers, they were given large discounts and shipped across the country. These guns, percussion and cartridge, rifle, carbine, and pistol, were then sold for a fraction of the original value. Cap-and-ball revolvers could often be found for less than $10. Single shot rifles, often percussion fired, could also be found at discounts, also often costing less than one half of the cost of new, cartridge firing rifles.

It becomes apparent that most of the arms owned by skilled labor like cowboys were not the guns that supposedly either won or tamed the West. The guns used for many years were the earlier percussion guns. Even the likes of James "Wild Bill" Hickok carried a pair of 1851 Colt Navy pistols well into the era of cartridge firearms. He was even carrying them when he was killed in 1876—several years after the introduction of the large bore cartridge guns made by Colt, Smith & Wesson, and Remington.

Many stories of the West are just that—stories. In the case of the guns carried and the equipment used, many of the tales were dreamed up by marketing departments, salesmen, and pulp authors. We know that the cowboy carried a gun or two and that he had to use them on occasion, but the romantic vision of a man on a horse going on adventure after adventure is a fantasy that common sense easily dismisses.

THE NEXT WEST

THE US MODEL 1899 PHILIPPINE CONSTABULARY KRAG CARBINE

When most people think of the Wild West, they often think of cowboys driving their herds to market, miners looking for the mother lode of gold or silver, settlers crossing the unending prairie in their Conestoga wagons, and soldiers and Indians fighting it out during the Plains Wars. What few people think to examine can be summed up by the question: Where do these people go when the Frontier is no more? Eventually, trains took the place of cattle drives, the veins of ore ran out or were controlled by large companies, the useable land was taken, and a peace, of sorts, was reached.

In 1893, a historian from the University of Wisconsin stated at a conference of the nation's historians that the West was, effectively, closed. The historian, Frederick Jackson Turner, based his observation on data from the National Census of 1890. As a result of the number of people who had moved to the West, the region was "civilized" and that since the definition of "The West" had been the uncivilized region west of the Mississippi River, it no longer existed as a point for historic discussion. With nowhere for the Western population to go and no new area to settle, there was no more "Frontier." Although this presentation was not the cause for the events of the next decade, it gave an example of some of the crisis of purpose that the nation was experiencing.

With little room for a continuation of the Frontier and a desire to create an empire, the United States took the excuse given by Spain's behavior in Cuba, Puerto Rico, and the Philippines Islands. In each of these areas, independence movements were causing problems for the Spanish who held these lands as part of their empire. Under the pretext of monitoring the situation, the USS Maine, flagship of the American fleet was sent to Cuba where it anchored in Havana Harbor. After an accidental explosion in one of the Maine's coal bunkers, relations between the United States and Spain quickly spiraled out of control and on April 25 (retroactive to April 22), 1898, the United States declared war on Spain.

As war fever again swept the country, federal troops and the various state militia organizations swung into action. Although the state units were mostly armed with the venerable Springfield Trapdoor, the United States armed the federal troops with a new rifle that claimed several firsts with its adoption. It was the first repeater, the first bolt action, the first foreign-designed, and the first smokeless cartridge rifle to be in service with the US military. The Krag-Jorgensen rifle, developed in Denmark and adopted by the United States in 1892,

IN 1893, A HISTORIAN FROM THE UNIVERSITY OF WISCONSIN STATED AT A CONFERENCE OF THE NATION'S HISTORIANS THAT THE WEST WAS, EFFECTIVELY, CLOSED.

US Model 1899 Krag-Jorgensen Philippine Constabulary Rifle

was a huge break in tradition. The previous four decades had seen the American military refuse to consider any firearm that was capable of repeating fire. It was rare for any nation, much less a fledgling world power, to adopt a firearm that was developed in a foreign country.

Within four months, the Spanish had surrendered and abandoned Cuba, Puerto Rico, and the Philippine Islands. The American government (and industry) saw Cuba and Puerto Rico as protectorates and the means to expand regional control. It was a different situation in the Pacific. The American government told the Filipino natives that they would receive self-rule after the Spanish turned over control. When this failed to happen, the pre-existing insurrection against the Spanish became an insurrection against the American rulers. This insurrection lasted until 1902, although the army continued to fight Moro rebels for many years after this. Regardless of that outcome, the Philippines never did lose American control until after the Japanese invasion of the islands in 1941.

The Wild West aspect of this long period of violence involved the initial American plans in 1898. While many of the volunteers for the Spanish-American War wished to fight in the much nearer Cuban theater–less than 100 miles from Florida–many of the Westerners ended up destined to fight in the Philippines. These soldiers from California, Colorado, Montana, Utah, Wyoming, and elsewhere, were Westerners in the truest sense of the word. They were cowboys, lumberjacks, and miners, for the most part. Looking for glory and a chance to prove their worth as men, many of these troops were also in search of riches.

Many of the nation's newspapers printed and reprinted articles on the various aspects of Spain's holdings as a travelogue of sorts. Among the facts presented was information concerning the various economic strong points of these areas. For example, many of the miners from Colorado and Montana who signed up did so with full knowledge of the mining opportunities in the Philippines. A full third of the Montana volunteers decided to stay in the Philippines after their planned tour of duty, presumably to make their fortune in the new Frontier, well to the west of the West they knew.

After the American army was successful in their attempt to "civilize 'em with a Krag", Filipinos performed most basic security work. The weapon they were issued was the final version of the Krag-Jorgensen—the Model 1899 Philippine Constabulary Carbine. Essentially the same rifle as its predecessors, this rifle still used the same .30-40 cartridge. Although the Krag was an improvement over the rifles used previously and a move in the same direction then being taken by many European armies, it was already falling behind. The .30-40 cartridge, underpowered in comparison, helped lead to the Krag's replacement by the US Model 1903 rifle, which used a larger .30 caliber cartridge that led to the development of today's .30-06 cartridge.

PART V

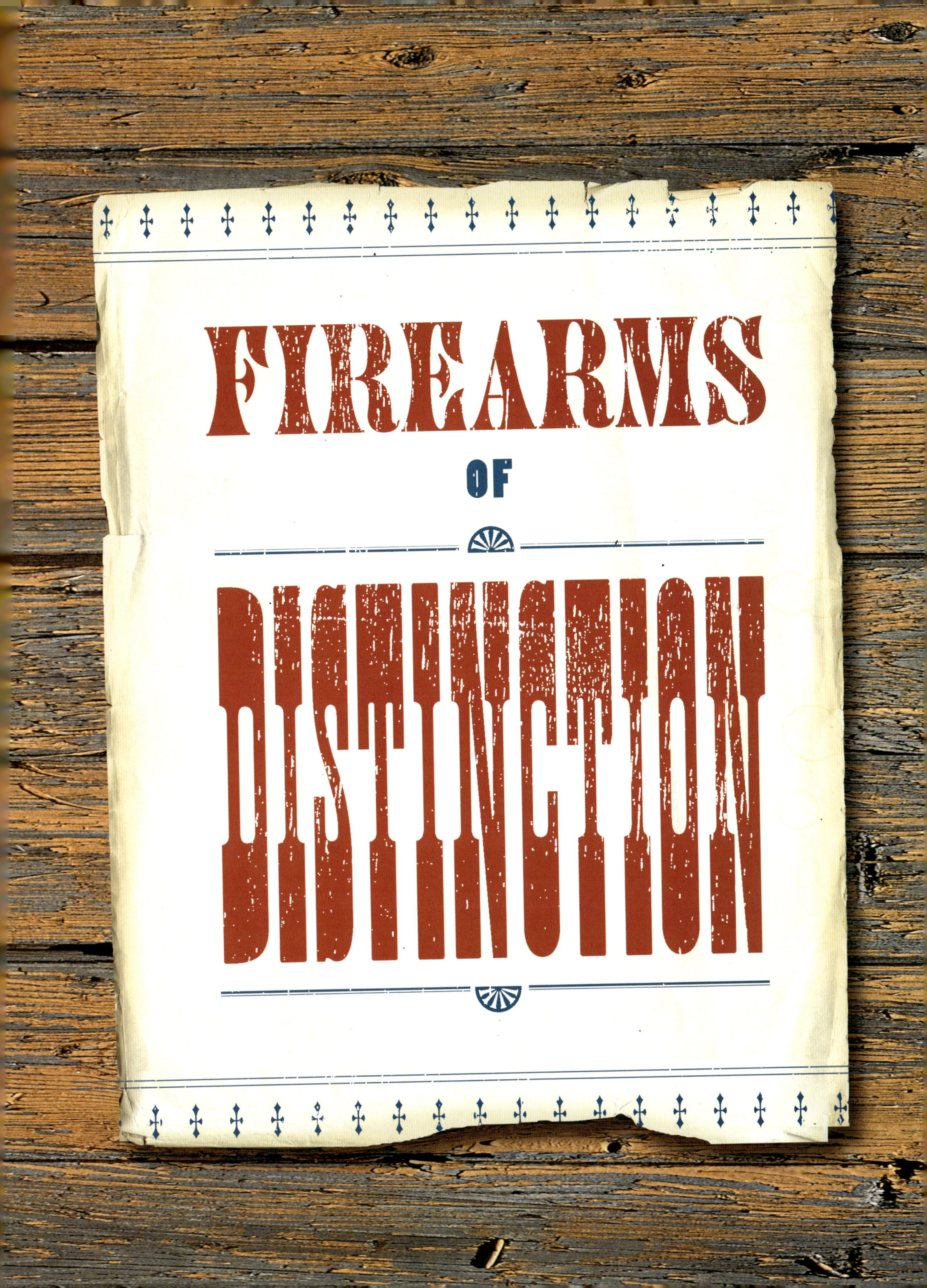
FIREARMS
OF
DISTINCTION

Schuetzen Style Rifle made by Joseph Meunier

GERMAN BEER, GERMAN GUNS

MEUNIER SCHUETZEN RIFLE

While the history of the American firearm industry is seen by many to have originated with German-Americans living in Pennsylvania, Germanic involvement in American firearms has continued intermittently into the 21st century. Militarily, the US Model 1903 rifle was effectively an unlicensed copy of the German Mauser. As the 21st century begins, the US military is again looking to Germany for a new rifle design. As for civilian shooting, the German pastime of holding Schuetzenfests (Shooting Festivals) took hold in every center of Germanic migration within the West, affecting firearms design in certain regions.

The Germans who moved west were, for the most part, members of two social classes. Whereas the Irish, Chinese, and African-Americans were often seen as laborers and the English were often among the upper-class, the Germans were often craftsmen or farmers. A large number of these immigrants combined their skills from these two areas and opened up many of the small breweries throughout the West.

From Cincinnati to Wisconsin to Denver, German immigrants who congregated in any numbers for holidays took the opportunity to hold marksmanship competitions. These schuetzenfests were part social gathering and part serious sporting event. Attracting competitors in the hundreds and crowds in the thousands, these were the social events of the year. The prizes could be worth hundreds of dollars and the winners could become minor celebrities.

The tools used in these competitions were high quality firearms that were specialized for this type of competition. Generally no larger than .38 caliber, and usually only firing .22 bullets, these rifles were commonly custom built for individual shooters. With highly carved, form-fitting stocks and pommel grips under the barrel, they were specifically meant for off-hand shooting—that is, shooting from a standing position with no support other than the shooter's own body. At ranges of 100 to 200 yards, expert marksmen could place a dozen bullets in the area covered by a quarter.

The heavy, octagonal barrels ensured that the rifles could retain their accuracy after repeated firing. The sights were highly accurate and capable of the very finest adjustment. The triggers were generally in a very sensitive double-set configuration, allowing the shooter to discharge the firearm with only the slightest touch of the front trigger after first setting the action with a pull of several pounds on the rear trigger.

The Schuetzen rifle pictured here was custom made by Joseph Meunier for Philip Best. Best founded the Best Brewing Company in Milwaukee, Wisconsin. This company is still around, although under another name. Best's oldest daughter, Maria, married Frederick Pabst, a local German resident who worked for Best and later took over the brewery, giving it his own name. Best's Meunier went to his son-in-law and then stayed in the Pabst family for several generations.

The gun maker Meunier, was considered by many to be one of the master craftsmen of the era. This Meunier rifle with a percussion action has a number of special design features, including a hammer in the shape of a breaching dolphin. While this rifle was of a special quality and very expensive, it is an example of the sort of work demanded by and affordable to those of the social class shared by Best, Adolph Coors, and other major brewers.

These guns would have been owned partially as display pieces, but first and foremost to allow them to compete against their employees in schuetzenfests sponsored by the brewery. Adolph Coors was one of several gentlemen who went so far as to collect firearms used in and around Golden and Denver, Colorado. The Coors Collection of Schuetzen Arms represents both ordinary and special firearms used by the German citizens of

Schuetzen Style Rifle
made by Joseph Meunier

Colorado during the late 1800s. Among the highly customized arms in the collection are Stevens and Maynards that were all originally designed as serious target rifles.

A number of the design elements that were standard among schuetzen arms are still in use for custom firearms. The double set trigger is standard on guns meant for varmint hunting or long range shooting. High quality, finely tunable iron sights are still in use by collegiate and Olympic target shooters. Rifle stocks specifically built for individual shooters are a standard aspect of individually fitted rifles for the wealthy shooter who wishes to spare no expense. In addition to the firearm developments, there were also tightened community bonds.

These German-Americans were part of the bedrock on which the growth of civilization in the West started. Whether as skilled workers in the mechanical arts and brewing, or as farmers spread across the West, the impact of their work affected society by making it more stable. Part of this stability was the social network established by these communities. This social network was made all the stronger as a result of the Schuetzenfests held across the country.

THE LAST GUN OF A MOUNTAIN MAN

A COLT FRONTIER MODEL REVOLVER

In late 1883, a pistol was shipped out from Hartford, Connecticut's, Colt's Patent Fire Arms Manufacturing Company. Based on engraving on the backstrap, it was ordered by Major W. M. Dunn, US Army, who gave it to Thomas T. Tobens in 1883.

The pistol is a Colt Model 1878 "Frontier" double-action revolver (meaning you do not have to cock the hammer in order to fire the pistol), serial number 11689. Obviously having seen use, the pistol is chambered for .45 Colt, one of the most popular cartridges of the period. The two aspects of the gun that makes it stand out are the embellishment and the background. It is heavily engraved, appearing to be in the style of longtime Colt employee Cuno Helfricht, and has ivory grip panels simply etched in a diamond pattern. According to records cited by the author Larry Wilson, this is one of approximately 200 embellished "Frontier" model pistols. That it is inscribed makes it more rare. The inscription, "MAJOR W.M. DUNN U.S.A. TO THOMAS T. TOBENS 1883," contradicts the nature of an embellished arm, especially when looking at the distressed condition of this pistol.

Colt Model 1878 "Frontier" given to Tom Tobens

According to Heitman's Historical Register and Dictionary of the United States Army, a William McKee Dunn served as an artillery officer in the US Army. At the time of his assignment to the 2nd Artillery Regiment in 1870, he was listed as a captain. In 1891, he is listed as a Major with the 3rd Artillery Regiment. As both of these units were represented in the Colorado area during the period, it is possible that this is the soldier named on the backstrap.

The recipient of the pistol, Thomas Tate Tobin (one of at least 4 different spellings of his last name), was born in St. Louis in 1823 of an Irish father and either a Canadian or Indian mother. In the 1840s, he relocated to the New Mexico frontier as a mountain man. Over the next 30 years, he would earn quite a reputation for his skills in the wilderness and with a Hawken rifle. He spent time with Charles Bent, Ceran St. Vrain, and Kit Carson in New Mexico and Colorado—Carson's son, William, later married one of Tobin's daughters. In 1847, he joined St. Vrain's Company of Mountain Men, raised to help quell the Taos uprising of Mexicans and Indians spurred by the seizure of New Mexico by the United States.

His claim to fame was the tracking, and later killing, of the Espinosa brothers in 1863. The Espinosa brothers were the sons of a Mexican landowner in New Mexico, and were believed responsible for a rash of killings in southern Colorado during the spring of that year. Tobin, accompanied by two soldiers from Fort Garland, Colorado, and a Mexican boy, tracked the two brothers to their camp. In the ensuing gunfight, Tobin killed both brothers. After this high point, Tobin's life was relatively sedate (barring an almost fatal gunfight with his son-in-law). He remained in the area around Fort Garland, already his home for many years. He died at home in 1904.

The year mentioned on the pistol—1882—was eventful only in that the US Army closed Fort Garland. This leads to a leap of logic (and a little bit of faith) that Tobin may have received this pistol as a gift as the result of service to the military community or perhaps, simply, a sign of friendship. Regardless of where it came from or why, this embellished revolver is an example of how a normally practical item can also be an impractical gift. The giver, a professional soldier, and the recipient, a hunter of animals and men, were both familiar with guns as a tool, not as a piece of art that would simply sit on a shelf, as embellished arms usually did. One of the few things not known was if these two men understood the irony of the situation—two shooters involved with a gun that was never intended to be fired.

POLITICS, GUNS, AND GIFTS

A WINCHESTER MODEL 1886 RIFLE

One of the guiding forces behind the shaping of the West has always been politics. The elected and appointed officials in Washington, D.C., have always been as important to the West as those individuals who lived there. From the members of Congress to the President, the power brokers on the Potomac River affected the lives of those in the West in many ways. From geography to transportation to industry, Federal decisions carried great weight—and great rewards. Gifts, employment, and power often rewarded those in the West who were able to support the victor in any particular campaign.

Presidential influence alone changed much in the West. Jefferson ordered the first major expedition in the West, sending Lewis and Clark to the Pacific Ocean. The nation's belief in "Manifest Destiny", a term coined by the journalist John L. O'Sullivan, validated westward expansion at almost any price. Zachary Taylor's resulting, and unpopular, Mexican-American War added the areas now known as Arizona, California, Nevada, Utah, and parts of Colorado, New Mexico and Wyoming. Lincoln's prosecution of the American Civil War was as much about the future of the American West as it was about the North and South. There were many changes that originated from the White House.

Winchester Model 1886 Rifle given by Theodore Roosevelt to James Owens

Winchester Model 1886 Rifle given by Theodore Roosevelt to James Owens

One of the farthest-reaching and longest-lasting changes that took place in the West was the creation of the National Forest System. This change took place in 1907 at the hand of Theodore Roosevelt, hero of the Spanish-American War, former Secretary of the Navy, and former governor of New York. While President, Roosevelt took action on a topic that was near and dear to his heart—wilderness conservation. During his tenure Roosevelt set aside 230 million acres under federal protection as parks, monuments, preserves, and national forests. The national forests obviously represented the lion's share of these spaces. With the assistance of Gifford Pinchot, Roosevelt set aside 150 million acres of wilderness as National Forests, bringing these areas under federal management. Most famous was the creation of the "Midnight Forests" in the Western United States as a response to business interests in Congress hamstringing Roosevelt's other attempts to protect areas that could be exploited for financial gain. Prior to signing into law a bill that would prevent the President from setting land aside in this manner without approval of Congress, he did just that by setting aside 17 million acres across the West.

The causes of this action were Roosevelt's long experience with and love of the outdoors. While some authors and historians have looked at Roosevelt and other early conservationists as wanting to preserve nature at all costs by changing nothing, many of these figures were quite different. The vast majority of the conservationists of the 19th and early 20th centuries were civic-minded businessmen, understanding the need to preserve wilderness areas while managing them to a certain extent as resource areas for industry. These gentlemen were, with few exceptions, hunters, anglers, or both. Roosevelt was the epitome of this movement, taking the middle path between the extremes of a pristine, untouched wilderness and a "tamed" and managed area that was once wild.

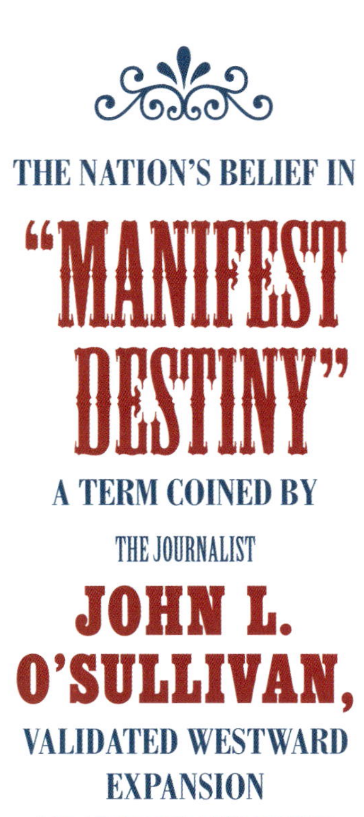

Roosevelt had been an outdoorsman for most of his life. Slowed down by asthma as a child, his father instilled in him a love of the outdoors, an appreciation for all things wild, and the joys of hunting and fishing. Part of this education involved exercise and strenuous activity to strengthen the body and the mind. Later in life he had an opportunity to experience "the strenuous life" firsthand on a ranch in Medora, Dakota Territory (now North Dakota) and as a hunter in the Dakotas, Idaho, Montana, Wyoming, and elsewhere. It was during this period and later that Roosevelt received informal training in conservation through correspondence with Pinchot, George Bird Grinnell, and others.

However, even with a belief system such as his and the money to back it, he would not have succeeded in any of these goals had it not been for the network of supporters behind him. One of these supporters was James Owen, a politician from Denver, Colorado. Owens was a lawyer, judge, legislator, and a powerful figure in Colorado. This position allowed him to provide tangible support for Roosevelt in the state. As with modern politics, the relationship would last only as long as there were benefits to both parties. In this case, one of the benefits to Owen was the receipt of a Winchester Model 1886, the premier lever-action hunting rifle of its day.

ART AND EMBELLISHMENT

A WINCHESTER MODEL 1866 RIFLE

One of the easiest methods of understanding any period of human history is through the study of the period's art. This is equally true of Asian, European, Mesoamerican, and African history. One of the most telling aspects of a culture's art is in the decorative arts. The materials used as a base for decoration, the patterns and designs rendered in the surface, and any other materials introduced into the art can each give meaning to the final product. This art can then help to build a clear picture of the artist, the patron, and the society that produced the work. When looking at the American West, embellished firearms can add to this picture of the period and its people.

With the earliest growth of the arts in the American Colonies, engravers and other metal-workers were among the crème de la crème of the period's artisans. These artisans were responsible for engraving everything from fine silver to firearms. The early firearms were often marked with symbols from various pagan and Christian traditions, Masonic organizations, and nature. The use of these symbols showed the participation with organizations. It was believed that the naturalistic symbols were able to imbue the firearm and its owner with unnatural abilities while hunting. As time progressed, newer symbols came into use as events occurred, incorporating images from the growing move for independence and other designs used solely for decoration. The settlers of the "early West"—the Ohio River Valley—often carried decorated arms of this type.

Winchester Model 1866, Engraved by Conrad Ulrich

The combination of the Industrial Revolution and westward expansion affected the types of guns carried in the West. Mass production, initiated by the military and adopted by the civilian arms industry, took hold in the Connecticut River Valley and led to a change in the basic characteristics of the arms produced. Where each rifle, pistol, and shotgun was carved and worked by hand, every part of a firearm was now forged, cut, and shaped by machine. Every lock, stock, and barrel was, essentially, identical. With the intention of selling as many guns as possible, artistry took a back seat. The only way to own a customized firearm, especially if this customization involved engraving, inlay, or a special finish, was to spend more money on a special order.

Costing anywhere from five to fifty dollars, engraving was a special touch that became the mark of a gentleman's gun. Not expected of a run-of-the-mill hunting gun or sidearm, a little bit of decoration transformed a plain gun from the assembly line into a work of art. Each of the major manufacturers and many smaller companies had their own artists working in-house to perform these tasks. Among the more famous engravers were Gustave Young, Cuno Helfricht, W. H. Gough, and the various members of the Ulrich family. Working as factory engravers for

Colt, Winchester, Smith & Wesson, and others these artists also performed contract work for other companies and private individuals. With the education and training received by these men—firearms engraving was not a trade often experienced by women—a high quality of work was not only understandable, but also expected.

The majority of the successful American engravers of the late 1800s were usually born and raised in Germany. In order to be considered a serious engraver, these immigrants were expected to have been accomplished artists in their home countries or to have been trained by a master engraver in the United States. The product of the centuries-old practice of apprenticeship at the hands of master craftsmen, certain skilled artists of the guild houses of Europe were able to achieve a high level of success in the United States. This success was limited to a relatively small group of engravers as this decoration was not as suitable in much of the Americas as it was in Europe. A large percentage of European civilian arms received special treatment by artists, in large part due to the stable nature of the lifestyle. As with New England, much of the European sporting population would return to their homes in the evening, allowing their arms to be cared for and stored in conditions befitting an embellished arm. In the American West, a residential or stable population was in the minority for many years, limiting the conditions conducive to ownership of a special firearm. As a result, the job field for arms engravers was not as open in the Americas. Those engravers who worked for the firearms companies were often the best in their trade.

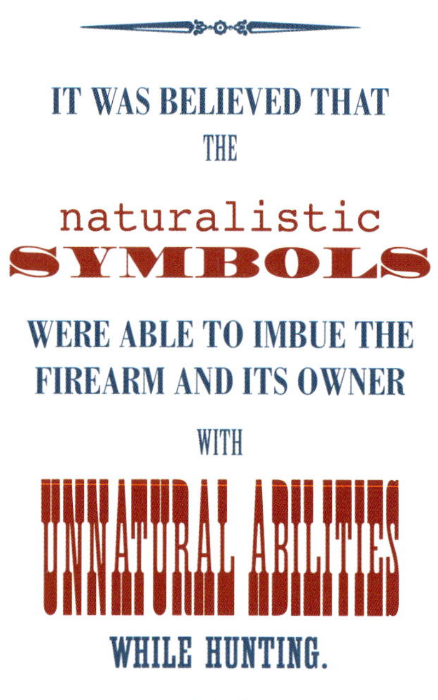

The engraving shops of the 1800s and those seen today are eerily similar. Workmen using jeweler's loupes are hunched over work tables crammed together in a small space. Drawings of various intricate designs hang above the tables and, beneath racks of tools, firearms parts are arrayed in an order understood by the artists. The designs are often similar, if not identical, to those that were in the engravers' pattern books of a century ago. In this respect, firearms engraving is an oddity. While the other branches of the decorative arts have followed other movements, such as Art Nouveau, Arts and Crafts, Art Deco, and Modern, firearms engravers have generally stayed in the gothic-related designs prevalent in the late 1800s. While there are a few modern firearms engravers who break this mold—Paul Lantuch of Sturm, Ruger, and Company, most notably—there is barely a market for designs and patterns that are not reminiscent of those seen at the turn of the 20th century.

The various uses of a gun are often apparent by knowing the type and caliber. Knowing this information allows the viewer to interpret the possible region of the country (or world) and social class of the user. The embellishing of an arm can often aid in this. The amount of engraving seen can help to determine the initial value of an arm or the purpose. Any animals, objects, or people in a design can help to determine the pastimes and hunting goals of a firearm owner. Lastly, the condition of the arm can be used to infer if the firearm remained with the purchaser and his or her descendants or if it simply became a tool for another. Every firearm had a use and a purpose. The use of embellishment can aid in the understanding of the this use and purpose, thereby giving an insight into the period of manufacture and the owner of, in some cases, a work of art.

Winchester Model 1887 Shotgun, given to Harvey Firestone by Henry Ford

TRADE AND TRANSPORTATION

A WINCHESTER MODEL 1897 SHOTGUN

The death of the "Wild West" can be attributed to many things, among them the expansion of the railroad network across the West, the arrival of civilization in its many forms, and the establishment of orderly and safe societies. In reality this progression merely led to a rural society that was, and is, still as wild as it could be. It is not unheard of to see locals ride horses into bars or to fire off their guns into the ceiling of that same bar or at the town's streetlights. While events such as these are still few and far between, they are still considered to be representative of the West that was.

The final nail in the West's coffin came from the unlikely location of Detroit, Michigan, where Henry Ford started production of his Model A in 1903. The use of the same assembly line techniques seen in the stockyards of Chicago or, earlier, in the firearms factories of the Connecticut River Valley, saw the Ford Motor Company revolutionize their production starting in 1913. The effects of this mass production of cars did not show in the West immediately. Besides the lack of maintained roads, early gasoline-powered autos needed a source of fuel in the nation's hinterlands. And neither the gasoline- or steam-powered cars of the turn-of-the-century had the horsepower or cargo capacity to be competitive with the old standard—the horse and wagon.

With the end of World War II, the West saw an influx of emigrants from the urban areas of the country. Additionally, many people began to travel the West in cars purchased during the relative affluence of the postwar period. The introduction of the Interstate Highway System created during the Eisenhower administration put the final touches on the expansion of civilization. Interstate trucking, ease of travel, and urbanization along the lines of the "fly-over" states' major highways have changed the West.

THE FINAL NAIL IN THE WEST'S COFFIN CAME FROM THE UNLIKELY LOCATION OF DETROIT, MICHIGAN.

Two of the important individuals behind the origination of this growth were the aforementioned Henry Ford and the chief executive of an important and directly related corporation—Firestone. As the major source of tires used in Ford's early autos, the two transportation magnates influenced the industry in design, manufacture, and sales. The cooperation between Ford and Firestone directly affected many aspects of modern life, including, but not limited to economics, food production, and even civil order.

Winchester Model 1887 Shotgun, given to Harvey Firestone by Henry Ford

This close relationship can be seen in a Winchester Model 1887 lever-action shotgun. The Model 1887, one of the earliest repeating shotguns in widespread use and one of many invented by John Browning, was a popular gun in many quarters. It commonly came in both 10 and 12 gauge, allowing hunters to use it against a variety of game. Many other citizens of the West—law enforcement, jailers, rail and stage guards, and ranch hands—were all users of the 1887. It was also popular among criminals as it offered more firepower than a double barrel shotgun and it could be easily concealed if the barrel was shortened

John Ulrich engraved the shotgun shown here, serial number 1, in order for Winchester to use it as a presentation piece for exhibit at the various expositions and World's Fairs of the period.

Eventually this gun caught the eye of Henry Ford, who purchased this shotgun as a gift for Harvey Firestone, helping to cement their business relationship. Gifts like this were par for the course in the business world of the period, making today's corporate gifts of pens and coffee mugs look paltry by example.

The relationships in business helped to build America. In more areas than just the automotive world, relationships paid off. Mine owners, cattlemen, and timber men all had relationships of this sort with the corporate officers of the railroads. The railroad officers had friends in the government. The Government officials had friends everywhere. In a period before any semblance of corporate responsibility, gifts flowed, favors were asked, and backs were patted. The end result was that the West changed and eventually became less wild.

"MODERN" MANUFACTURE

A WINCHESTER MODEL 1873 "1 OF 1000"

Many people in the firearms industry are proud of modern firearms. They can go on for hours about the modern use of stainless steel and polymers, recoil-dampening modifications, high quality optics, modern manufacturing techniques, and the use of robotics. If asked about the firearms of the 1800s, many of these same people will immediately begin to describe the failures of the antiques. Pointing to a lack of quality control, supposedly archaic manufacturing techniques and shoddy workmanship, lack of technological expertise, an inability to use modern ammunition, and the use of wood, iron, and, later, steel, they may use words like "quaint," "interesting," and even "dangerous." This description is not completely true.

By the 19th century, the manufacturing industry had reached the point of using steam power in the various factories of Europe and the Americas. For the manufacturing of textiles, the steam power allowed quick and relatively easy work. This mass production moved much of the economy from small shops to large factories and the transition from the artisan to the worker. Although creativity was not valued, the product quality was, on average, better than the cottage industry could provide.

It was because of the earlier modernization of the textile industry that the firearms industry thrived. As with textiles, there was a need for mass-produced identical firearms. The world's militaries needed hundreds of thousands of arms for their troops. With the preternatural ability of the average soldier to ruin equipment, repairs to these arms needed to be simple, using interchangeable parts. In few other areas was there such a need for this level of standardization. Prior to this time any object made from wood or metal was an individual, being completely different from any other object of the same type. Technology, a combination of

BY THE TIME OF THE **AMERICAN CIVIL WAR,** THE FIREARMS IN USE WERE BUILT FROM TRULY **INTERCHANGEABLE PARTS.**

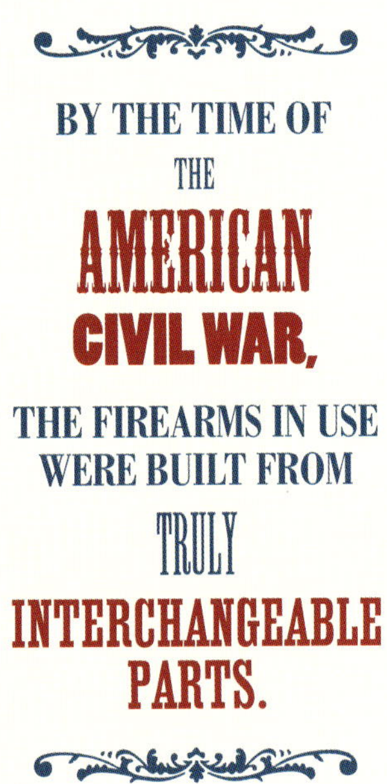

power and the knowledge, starting in the 1820s, introduced interchangeable parts, quality standards far surpassing those seen previously, and mass production on a level not previously seen in any mechanical field.

While historians have looked at the car industry or meat industry as developing the assembly line process in manufacturing, the firearms industry truly developed this process. With each employee focusing on a specific component, rather than an entire firearm, the cost—in time and money—of the manufacturing process decreased. While the artistic merits of the finished products left something to be desired, the tolerances, standardization, and durability of the finished products were greater than those seen in the days of the small shops and smithies. By the time of the American Civil War, the firearms in use were built from truly interchangeable parts. With the advances in production methods, both the quantity and quality of the arms produced was much higher than seen previously. This fact, combined with the location of the vast majority of America's firearms industry in the Connecticut River Valley, has been shown in many histories to have been one of the major factors in the final resolution of the Civil War.

One of the companies that evolved from a supplier to the Union Army was the Winchester Repeating Arms Company. Oliver Winchester, originally a shirt maker who saw the strengths of the firearms industry and the New Haven Arms Company, bought controlling interest in the

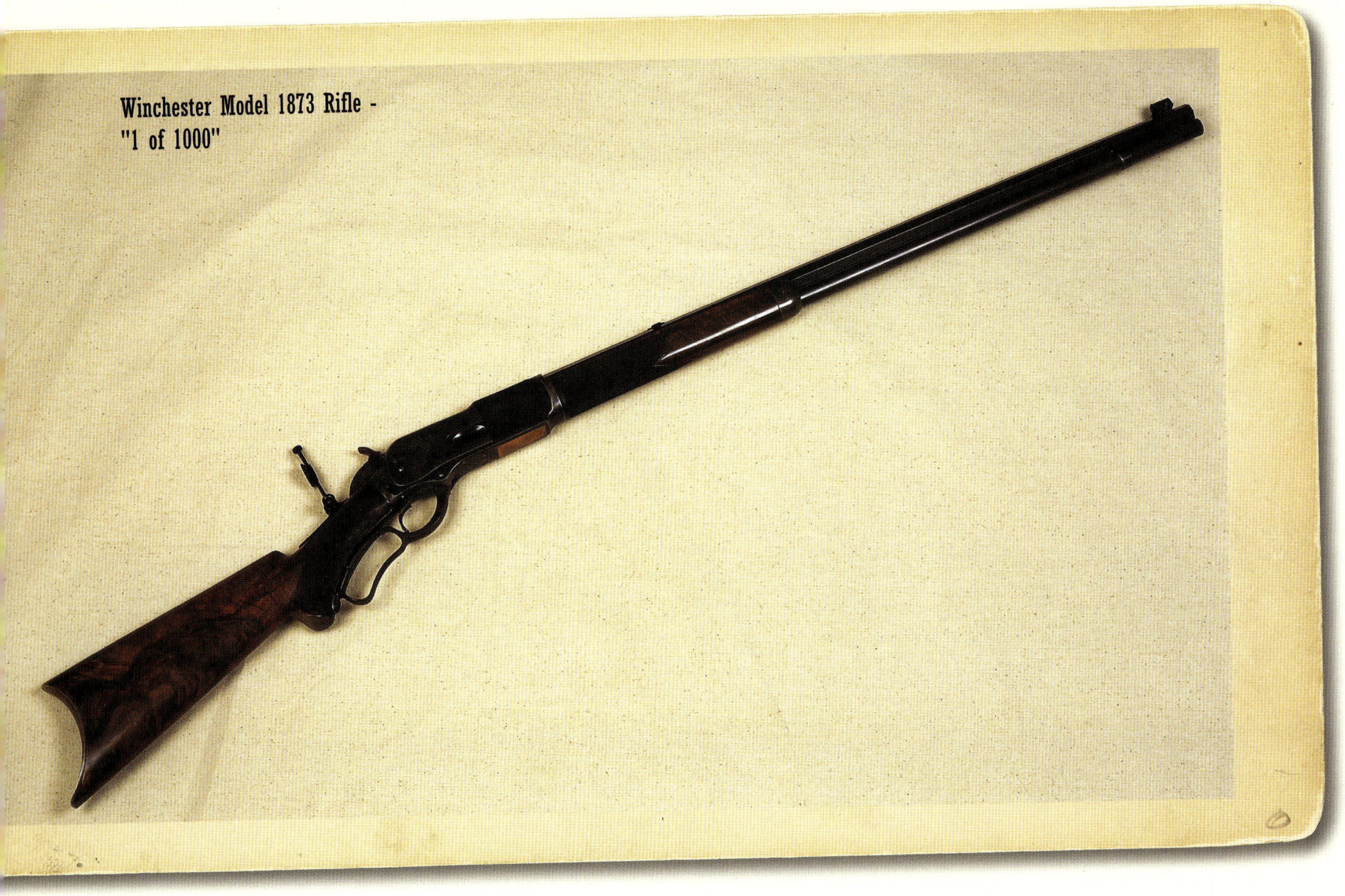

Winchester Model 1873 Rifle - "1 of 1000"

company, and changed the name. While the Winchester name is now well known as manufacturing the Model 1873, "The Gun That Won the West", the company's first activity after the Civil War was to market an improved version of its primary civilian arm, the 1866, to various militaries in Europe and the Americas. Although this was a failure, the resulting design modifications led to the introduction of the new rifle in 1873.

The Winchester 1873, the famed rifle of numerous stories and at least one star-studded film, was a technological masterpiece—one of many during the period. The quality of the period's firearms was, in many ways, similar to that of the arms produced today. In fact many of the companies currently building firearms are still using methods and machines developed in the last quarter of the 19th century. Many of the firearms from this period are still in use, showing the effects of careful maintenance and storage.

One historical aspect of the Model 1873 that shows the capabilities of 19th century production is the "1 of 1000." As with all quality production firearms, Winchester test-fired each of their firearms. Some of this testing is to make sure that the firearm in question is safe, even with a cartridge loaded with too much propellant. Beyond the safety testing, accuracy testing took place as well. In the case of the Model 1873, the tester fired ten shots at a target. If the ten shots formed a small enough group, the rifle was called a "1 of 1000."

This classification as a "1 of 1000" led to the rifle being set aside and fitted with everything from a set trigger to fancy wood and sights. Winchester increased the price of the rifle from the $40 that was standard to $100. Over the course of the Model 1873 production cycle, 136 guns qualified for "1 of 1000" status. An additional 8 qualified for the lesser "1 of 100" status. This same classification was also used for the Model 1876 rifle with 54 "1 of 1000" rifles and 8 "1 of 100" guns. It is probable that the latter designation was not given as often as was appropriate, as, statistically, there had to be more guns with this degree of accuracy.

WHILE HISTORIANS HAVE LOOKED AT THE CAR INDUSTRY OR MEAT INDUSTRY AS DEVELOPING THE ASSEMBLY LINE PROCESS IN MANUFACTURING, THE FIREARMS INDUSTRY TRULY DEVELOPED THIS PROCESS.

Aside from the technology used in building firearms, there are few changes between the firearms industry of 1873 and today. While Winchester and others made their names mass-producing arms for the world, the products from the better companies were on par with today's top-of-the line firearms in quality. As with today's market, there were the knock-offs and cheap handguns affordable to the lower classes. While some construction tolerances are now improved with robotic Computer Numeric Control (CNC) machining techniques, the fit and finish of the guns carried in the West in the 1800s was as good as the guns of the 21st century. The "1 of 1000" is an example of this.

Winchester Model 1876, exhibited at the 1876 Philadelphia Exposition

CELEBRATIONS AND SALES

A WINCHESTER MODEL 1876

Manufacturing has always been a common theme in American History. The inability to produce finished goods was a bone of contention during the Colonial era. The early cottage industries of New England later gave way to the growth of the textile industry. This gave way to the mass production of mechanical goods. Then the majority of the American economy shifted from agriculture to manufacturing. Today the manufacturing of many goods may take place overseas, but there are still aspects of the various industries that have not changed. The need to advertise and sell goods has always been a factor in the success of a product. The act of advertising have changed but little in the last two centuries. The methods, on the other hand, have changed greatly.

The common methods of advertising products boil down to two types: word-of-mouth and direct advertising. Based on the quality of work performed, word-of-mouth advertising may or may not work, but it can be effective, depending on who is talking. Direct advertising, whether in posting bills in 18th century Boston or spending millions on a thirty-second commercial during the Super Bowl this year, has the same issues—it may or may not work, but it can be effective if done right. The easiest way for many manufacturers to spread the word about their products has always been through meeting their distributors or the end users of their products. Starting in the early 1800s in Europe, these meetings began to reach a grand scale as royalty began to host national expositions, essentially the predecessors of today's trade shows.

While these expositions were often nationalistic celebrations of a country's culture, industry, and arts, many exhibitors used them to their advantage to show off the company's products. This became especially true as the expositions began to be more inclusive, allowing the presentation of the products of other countries as precedents of World's Fairs. The London Exhibition of 1861 and the Paris Exposition of 1857 were two excellent examples of this as a number of American manufacturers were present. Among these were the various firearms manufacturers showing off their latest products. As with many of the successful ideas of Europe, America adopted the concept of the exposition for several important anniversaries in its own history.

Three specific celebrations were directly related to the growth of the United States, and subsequently of the West. The years 1876, 1893, and 1903, saw the celebrations of the nation's centennial, the 400th anniversary of Columbus' arrival in the Americas, and the centennial of the Louisiana Purchase. Held in Philadelphia, Chicago, and St. Louis respectively, these expositions gave the arms industry an opportunity to show off their wares to the public in a setting that celebrated the national spirit during each of these periods. The companies spared no expense in constructing their exhibits. The woodwork of the displays was the match of any New York show room, and the engraving and finish on the arms was the highest quality available. Some of these special arms exhibited at the various expositions sold to individuals and companies for large sums of money and, depending on the identities of the embellisher and the purchaser, these guns are often worth hundreds of thousands of dollars.

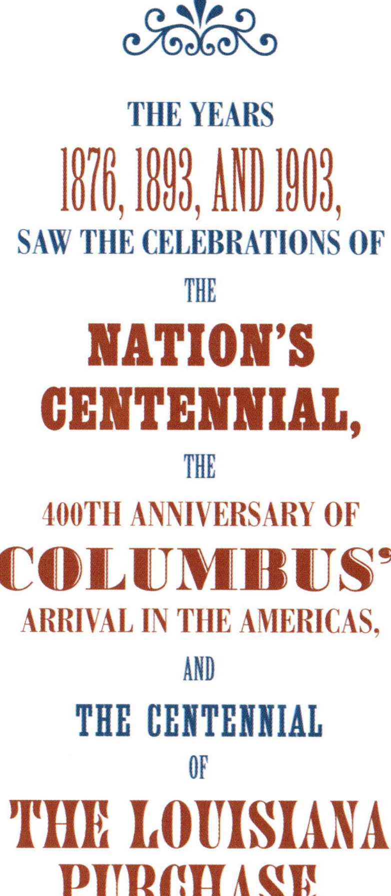

The 1876 Philadelphia Exhibition, celebrating the centennial of the nation's independence, saw the exhibition of what could be called the "class of '73"—the Colt Model 1873 Single Action Army revolver, the Winchester Model 1873 repeating rifle, and the US Model 1873 "Trapdoor" Springfield rifle. While the government-produced arms were not there for advertising, they were in the hands or on the shoulders of any soldiers present. The two civilian models of 1873, as well as a literal armory of other guns from Colt, Winchester, Smith & Wesson, Remington, Sharps, and other companies, represented the commercial arms. The timing of the Philadelphia Exposition was fortuitous, as the West was quickly adopting the newer cartridge firearms for the use of civilian and soldier alike. The establishment of the revolving pistol and the lever-action carbine and rifle as the chosen arms for cowboys and lawmen helped to establish their dominance for the next several decades. The large caliber single-shot rifle gained attention as a tool for both buffalo hunters and the target shooters of New England. The appearance of the US Model 1873 may have been anticlimactic in light of the defeat that summer of the 7th Cavalry at the Battle of the Little Bighorn in the Montana Territory, but it was just one more tool of Western expansion.

The Columbian Exposition was an important event in that the nature of technology was changing again, as was the national spirit. While many arms were still on exhibit, the designs were changing as bolt-action arms began to show up. Competitors to the Winchester rifle and the Colt revolver were on exhibit and America was coming to terms with the realization that the period of the Wild West was almost finished. This idea was all but proven that year by Frederic Jackson Turner's theory that the West was closed, because the 1890 Census listed the density of the West as having reached at least one person per square mile. Along with this change was a growing movement among the men of the middle and upper classes to seek adventure and strive to be more "manly" and live Roosevelt's "strenuous life" in order to "revitalize the race." As a result of this movement, the West no longer seemed good enough and the beginnings of an expansionist policy soon became apparent. This policy eventually led to a war and America's new "frontier" Territories.

The last of the three expositions mentioned here, the St. Louis Exposition of 1903, saw the introduction of arms that were undreamed of by Lewis and Clark one hundred years previously. With several major changes in firearms design and mass production, the arms available in the West were vastly different. In comparison, the arms of today are not quite so different. Few arms exhibited at the 1903 Exposition are still available from their original manufacturers—the Colt Single Action Army and the Winchester Model 1894 among the small group. Other arms are

Winchester Model 1876, exhibited at the 1876 Philadelphia Exposition

simply variations—relatives, if you will—of the arms exhibited. Today's Colt Automatic Pistol and its many clones are descendents of the Colt Models of 1900 and 1902. The US Model 1903, possibly seen in the hands of soldiers at that time, was the predecessor of Winchester and Remington's premier hunting rifles, the Model 70 and Model 700, respectively.

The Winchester Model 1876 shown in this chapter is an example of the arms built specifically for exhibition at major expositions and other shows. Believed to be the first Model 1876 manufactured, it has fancy wood, a pistol grip, a vernier sight, and is chambered for an experimental .50-40 cartridge. The advertising earned by companies at shows of this type helped to put the name of various companies in front of the gun-buying public. This advertising kept the success of the arms industry very much intertwined with the success of the American economy and America as a whole as the country grew in the late 19th and early 20th centuries.

WILLIAM F. "BUFFALO BILL" CODY SHOOTING HAND-THROWN TARGETS FROM HORSEBACK WITH A WINCHESTER MODEL 1873

PART
VI

REPRESENTATIONS
OF THE
WEST

William F. "Buffalo Bill" Cody, posed on horseback with a Winchester Model 1873 Rifle

THE GUNS OF BUFFALO BILL

Few stories of the West live up to the heroics set forth on stage and screen or in the pages of novels. This was, in many ways, a result of the need to market products. Whether or not they realized the stories were fictional, the audience of such works wanted to be entertained and surprised by the exploits of others. While many gunfighters and desperadoes of the Old West received fame and glory at the hands of dime-novel authors, some heroes of the period did it the old-fashioned way. Braving hostile environments, encountering wild animals and wilder men, and still finding their way out alive to tell the tale, these heroes were few and far between. William F. Cody became one of these heroes through his work and adventures in the West, though it was only through his showmanship that he gained the fame by which he is known today. This fame was brought about by Cody's use of firearms. Later this fame was used by others to make money off the Cody name.

Born in Iowa in 1846, Cody learned about hard work early in his life. By the age of 12, he was working on a wagon train, he was mining for gold at 13, and at 15 he rode for the Pony Express.

William F. "Buffalo Bill" Cody, posed with a Winchester Model 1873 Rifle and a pair of pearl-handled Colt revolvers

By the time he turned 20, he had scouted for the Union 7th Kansas Cavalry in the Civil War. In what was already an adventurous life, Cody continued to perform duties that set him apart from others. In his 20s he was a professional buffalo hunter for the Kansas Pacific Railroad, and he was a civilian scout and guide for the US Cavalry. It was during this work that the Army awarded Cody the Medal of Honor for actions taken during the Indian Wars, one of only four times that a civilian has received this award. It was also during this time that Cody met the likes of General Phil Sheridan, Lieutenant Colonel George Custer, and Russia's Grand Duke Alexis.

As a result of the attention given to Cody, he soon became the focus of dime-novels and was involved in stage shows about the West. Within ten years, he traded this interest in the West and his public persona into his fledgling touring company, known to us today as Buffalo Bill's Wild West. For 30 years, the Wild West show took Cody and his employees around the world, introducing him to presidents, royalty, and other heads of state. Crowds numbering in the thousands would show up to see Cody and his colleagues reenact famous battles, perform shooting exhibitions, and give an insight into the American West. The performances represented a romanticized version of events, but the overall effect educated the viewers in a manner not dissimilar to the newsreels of the early to mid 20th century.

One common aspect of each of the periods of Cody's life was the use of firearms. While the job, the location, and the friends and acquaintances changed, Cody regularly carried a gun.

William F. "Buffalo Bill" Cody posed with Indian Scouts

SEATED AT RIGHT William F. "Buffalo Bill" Cody holding his most famous rifle, "Lucretia Borgia"

The type of arm changed from time to time and task to task. One of the biggest misunderstandings about the famous personalities of the West is that they only had "their gun"—inferring that people of the period would buy a gun and keep it their whole life. While the term "disposable society" was invented in the recent past, the concept was alive and well in the Wild West. Gun owners regularly upgraded their arms and accoutrements as newer, better, and more dependable technologies were developed, or circumstances mandated the use of specific guns.

Although Bill Cody probably carried a small pocket pistol during his early travels and employment, the first firearm that would have been required by a job was likely a Colt Model 1849 Pocket Revolver or a Colt Model 1851 "Navy" Revolver. This revolver was Cody's sidearm during his stint as a rider for the short-lived Pony Express. With Cody's service in the 7th Kansas Cavalry, he would have been armed with a Sharps Carbine and a Colt Navy revolver. The standard long arm of the Union Cavalry, the Sharps would have most likely been Cody's first breech-loading arm. This would definitely not be his last.

FOR 30 YEARS, THE WILD WEST TOOK CODY AND HIS EMPLOYEES AROUND THE WORLD, INTRODUCING HIM TO PRESIDENTS, ROYALTY, AND OTHER HEADS OF STATE.

One interesting document found by historians shows that when leaving a position as a civilian scout after the Civil War, Cody apparently kept a US Model 1866 Springfield Rifle in his possession, effectively stealing it from the government. This breechloading rifle was a US Model 1863 Rifle, changed to the Second Allin Conversion. This model had the barrel modified in order accept and fire a .50-70 metallic cartridge. The design by Erskine Allin was the final conversion model before the introduction of the purpose-built "Trapdoor" Springfield rifles and carbines used by the military until the 1890s. This particular rifle became part of Western history in Cody's hands. Dubbed "Lucretia Borgia," due to it being so deadly, according to Cody, this rifle was Cody's primary firearm when he gained his nickname hunting buffalo for the Kansas Pacific Railroad.

William F. "Buffalo Bill" Cody

While no Springfield rifle was considered appropriate for buffalo hunting in the later era of buffalo hunting, it was a perfect match for the buffalo "runners" of Cody's era. Riding alongside the herd, Cody would fire into the shoulder of selected buffalo. The large bullet fired by the Model 1866 was capable of bringing down a buffalo in one shot while the smaller bullets fired by the repeaters used by many other hunters required two or more shots to produce the same effect. Over a seventeen-month period, Bill and Lucretia killed 4,280 head of buffalo in order to feed the railroad workers. After his work as a hunter, and a competition with another buffalo-hunting Bill—Bill Comstock—Cody earned the nickname "Buffalo Bill," the name by which he was known to millions later.

After another bout as a scout for the military, and the awarding of a Medal of Honor, Cody finally entered the world of show business. With occasional forays into the West as a guide for hunters and the military, Bill followed this lifestyle for four decades. His own show, Buffalo Bill's Wild West, ran for thirty years. It was during this time that Cody created what has become a most troublesome issue for gun historians, collectors, and well-meaning descendants. Cody made a habit of handing firearms out to many of the friends, acquaintances, and VIPs in his life. While many of these guns were engraved with the name of Cody and the recipient, untold numbers were simply handed out as gifts to local politicians and businessmen in the towns visited by the Wild West.

The problems that appeared as a result are that many of these guns cannot be verified as "Buffalo Bill" guns without a bill of sale or other identifying information. The easiest firearms to identify are guns that have been modified in some way to appear as belonging to Cody. Instead of a well-engraved "Col. William F. 'Buffalo Bill' Cody" on the gun (as is correct in most cases), the author has seen many attempts by bad engravers to replicate this theme. Many of these attempts look as if they were carved with a knife or screwdriver. Misspellings and other errors abound. One memorable case involved a revolver marked "F. William Cody." These poor fakes have caused no end of embarrassment to buyers of these guns or the descendants of individuals who were taken in by such stories.

Another area for fakery involves the guns used in Buffalo Bill's Wild West. The majority of the "working guns" used in the show, whether by Cody, Oakley, or others were smoothbore handguns and rifles, made to fire shot cartridges. Some dramatizations of this period interpret this in a bad light, making it seem that Cody needed to use shot cartridges to hit his targets. The true cause behind this is that many of the performances by the Wild West and other shows of the type were arrayed "in the round." This type of layout would guarantee fatalities at almost every performance if the performers used standard cartridges. The use of shot cartridges provided the desired effect while protecting the audience. Many guns have been sold as "Buffalo Bill Show Guns." Unfortunately, the "BB," "BBWW," or similar stamped letters followed with a supposed inventory number are fraudulent. The truth of the matter is that the performers in the show were required to provide their own firearms and that there were no company guns.

CODY MADE A HABIT OF HANDING FIREARMS OUT TO MANY OF THE FRIENDS, ACQUAINTANCES, AND VIPS IN HIS LIFE.

Throughout his life, Cody used a variety of rifles, from the Sharps and Springfields mentioned earlier to the newer Remingtons and Winchesters. While he is quoted as saying his Remington Rolling Block "Never failed me," he became more associated with Winchesters as his life went on. This is particularly true of the Model 1873, often seen in photographs and statues of Cody. He would typically use the arms he felt were appropriate. As with the other guns used in his life, he tended to go with what worked for the job at hand.

With Cody's death in 1917, it became obvious that an era was over. The West, for so long a springboard for those willing to make their mark on the world, or possibly die in the attempt, was becoming civilized. The challenges and opportunities were no longer as daunting and heroic. With the end of the first World War, the United States began to look to the future, rather than to the West. However, the legend of Buffalo Bill—and an unintended legacy of fraudulent firearms—lived on. During his life, he was probably the best-known person living—even in comparison to kings, queens, and presidents. Today he is still one of the best known historical figures of the West and the firearms he used represent the dynamic period.

Winchester Model 1892 Rifle owned by Annie Oakley

LITTLE SURE SHOT

ANNIE OAKLEY

On August 13, 1860, an unassuming girl was born in Ohio. As a result of the birth of Phoebe Ann Moses, the shooting world would never be the same. After growing up in a household that could be called dysfunctional at best, Annie—who always went by her middle name—would go on to become one of the most famous individuals in Western history, whether male or female. This fame would lead her to meet royalty, heads of state, and celebrities who thought it an honor to meet this girl from Ohio.

Annie Oakley Posing with a Stevens rifle and pistol, a Spencer slide-action shotgun, and an unidentified side-by-side shotgun

LEFT Annie Oakley Posing with a Marlin Model 1890, an unidentified side-by-side shotgun, a Smith and Wesson Model 3, and a Smith and Wesson single-shot target pistol

BELOW Winchester Model 1892 Rifle owned by Annie Oakley

Target shooting has not always been an equal opportunity sport. Until the 19th century, most women were not able to engage in the sport. Only the highest and the lowest classes were in positions that allowed them to shoot regularly for sport or for filling the cooking pot, depending on social class. Largely a man's sport and responsibility, shooting became a tacit symbol of the early equality movement. During the 1800s, this sport slowly opened to women. Although it was not until the mid-20th century that women with firearms were finally treated as something other than a novelty, there were many women who were able to enjoy this sport, whether out of desire or necessity.

Annie Moses was definitely someone who had to hunt out of necessity. The game she shot was sold to hotels and restaurants in the Cincinnati area, helping to support her family and eventually bringing them out of debt. Before she turned 16, Annie had achieved a modest level of fame amongst the businessmen of Cincinnati. This paid off when one of these businessmen invited Annie to take part in a shooting competition with a group of nationally-known shooters including Frank Butler. When everything was over, Annie had out-shot all of the touring marksmen. As a result, Butler became very attracted to this young girl, marrying her in 1876.

The 16-year-old Annie went on the road with Butler, not imagining the future they would have. After almost six years of marriage, Annie and Frank finally took the stage at the same time. From this point until her death in 1926, Annie would use the stage name of Oakley. The most famous period of this career, her tenure with Buffalo Bill's Wild West, took place from 1885 to 1901. This sixteen year run made "Annie Oakley" a household name and helped to introduce shooting to many women across the country and around the world. But this fame could not help during both the Spanish-American War and World War I as the Army turned down Oakley's offers to raise units of women volunteers. The Army declined her offers to teach recruits as a marksmanship instructor as well.

Annie's fame did lead to what may be one of the earliest attempts at product placement and corporate sponsorship. Many gun companies, both American and European, sent their products to Annie in the hopes that she would like their product and use it in her show. As Annie was a three-gun shooter—able to use handgun, rifle, or shotgun equally well—this led to a dizzying array of guns that showed up on her doorstep. Virtually every major and minor manufacturer raised their hopes only to have Annie dash them through stating on a pamphlet, "There is no such thing as the best gunmaker. 'The Best Gun' is the gun that best fits the shooter." This philosophy was apparent in her choice of arms. Depending on where she was and what she was shooting, Annie used Marlin and Winchester rifles, Smith & Wesson and Colt revolvers, and a variety of American and European shotguns. This collection, and the conscious decision to accept all guns as being relatively equal, is a perfect counterpoint to the incorrect belief in some quarters that every Western personality only had one gun—as in "What kind of gun did Annie Oakley use?" The appropriate answer to this question is "Most of them."

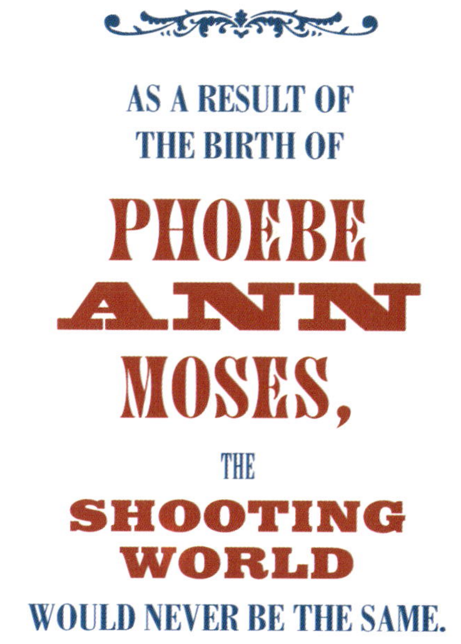

As a result of the many gifts and her tendency to use whichever gun worked best, Annie's gun collection at times contained an example of virtually every production gun of the period. There are even stories of her and other exhibition shooters using these free guns as gifts to other shooters and members of the public. In at least one case, Annie put an engraved Marlin rifle to good use by donating it to the government in order to raffle it off to help sell war bonds for World War I.

Although Annie Oakley had to hunt at first in order to support her family, she later succeeded with the abilities and skills she nurtured through her early "job" as a hunter. The experiences and adventures of her adult life were amazing considering her humble beginnings in Ohio. Her career was made all the more improbable by the simple nature of society. In a period before women received the vote, Annie Oakley represented all that women could do. She was independent, athletic, and famous in a period known for the restrictions placed on women by society. Her work as an exhibition shooter broke ground for others and encouraged generations of activists seeking women's rights.

Frederic Remington's Winchester Model 1894

THE WEST THROUGH ART

FREDERICK REMINGTON

The earliest wide-spread interpretations of the West by Europeans came in the form of drawings and paintings by the likes of Karl Bodmer and George Catlin. These art forms continued to be the medium by which many people found out about the West. Artists like Catlin presented their works (for a small fee) to the public in order to show the life and times of the frontier. Other artists were contracted by the government to take part in expeditions in order to "capture" the wilderness on paper or canvas. Thomas Moran accompanied such an expedition in 1871 in order to help the government consider what to do with the area soon to be declared as America's first national park. Moran's paintings, and images provided by the photographer William Henry Jackson, helped Congress decide to pass legislation naming Yellowstone as a national park. Once most of this exploratory era of the West was over, other artists began to capture images of the populated West. One of these artists, Frederick Remington, worked as a cowboy, traveled the West, and even traveled to Cuba as a reporter prior to the onset of the

Spanish-American war. During his career, Remington's work included two-dimensional and three-dimensional images that came to represent all that was the West. Not only did he create works that allowed others to view the West but also, as with the work of Catlin and Moran, his work affected those who followed later.

On his first trip to the West in 1881, Remington drew images of cowboys for publication in Harper's Weekly. Over the next two decades Remington drew pictures of soldiers, Indians, and other Westerners. His illustrations became popular fare in the magazines of the day, including Harper's and Collier's. These illustrations became very important to the many subscribers on the East Coast. As a welcome change from the fanciful adventures seen in the dime novels of the period, Remington's work showed the real West as it happened, not as it happened in a fiction writer's imagination.

Winchester Model 1894 Rifle owned by the artist Frederic Remington

Remington expanded his repetoire as an artist as time progressed. His work as an illustrator, the means to pay his bills, was soon supported by his work as a painter and sculptor. His work in these mediums took his illustrations to the next level, artistically and figuratively. His paintings, whether his earlier renderings of Western scenes or his later landscapes, always showed the true West, although with occasional attempts to show idealized interpretations of the period. Regardless, his paintings continued to influence those around him in New England. While many of his paintings and illustrations were relatively still, his sculpture was better suited to scenes that included at least some motion or activity. The tension and conflict shown were testaments to the situation Remington had seen in the West while traveling and learning of the challenges of living in the region west of the Mississippi River.

When not on his annual trips to the West, the artist spent much of his time at his studio in New Rochelle, New York, surrounded by artifacts collected during his travels, including a number of firearms. The arms were of two types—shooting arms and props. The many prop firearms ranged from ancient (even in Remington's day) flintlock pistols to Civil War-era percussion rifles to relatively modern Colt single action revolvers. Although they were often in various states of disrepair, Remington regularly used these arms when recreating Western scenes from his sketchbook.

REMINGTON'S WORK SHOWED THE REAL WEST AS IT HAPPENED IN TRUTH, NOT AS IT HAPPENED IN A FICTION WRITER'S IMAGINATION.

Remington's shooting arms were normally in fine condition. An avid hunter, Remington had learned the importance of quality arms during his time in the West. The Winchester Model 1894 Rifle pictured here, one of these quality arms, creates what is possibly the most difficult phrase to say in the English language (for a Gun Guy, that is)—Remington's Winchester. This particular gun was manufactured in 1897 and has some custom features which support the idea that this gun was not intended for the life of a prop. The pistol grip, half magazine, and checkered stock are all custom options that the manufacturer lists in the production record for this rifle. An odd feature of this Winchester is Remington's name literally scratched into the forestock. Although it does resemble the signature seen in Remington's created works, it would have been expected that Remington would have had his name engraved in the gun had it been a gift from Winchester or a patron or other acquaintance. This leads the author to believe that Remington bought this rifle for his own use and marked it in order to identify the owner. Regardless, it is safe to assume that Remington did use the rifle as it was returned for repair twice in a six month period during 1901.

Remington's work, quite distinctive in several ways, was a welcome vision of reality in a sea of nonsense that often produced a caricature of the true West. When seen in tandem with the work of Charlie Russell and others, a coherent interpretation of the West can be understood. This interpretation shows the work of the cowboy, the dreary existence of the cavalry soldier, and the often heartbreaking situation endured by the American Indian. Much more realistic than the more entertaining but factually inaccurate dime novels of the period, Western artists at the turn of the 20th century often painted a picture only slightly less accurate than the experience of the West, itself.

"SOMEDAY I'M GOING TO MARRY THAT MAN"

PLINKY TOPPERWEIN

In 1903, Elizabeth Servaty, a young woman working at Winchester's ammunition plant in New Haven, Connecticut, had a quick conversation with a demonstrator for the company that employed her. After he went off to a meeting, she turned to a coworker and told her, "Some day I'm going to marry that man." Later that year she followed through with this claim as she married Adolph Topperwein. This marriage changed the face of firearms exhibitions and firearms history, in general, for years to come.

Winchester Model 1903 Rifle, One of many firearms used by Plinky Topperwein

Although women had been involved in exhibition shooting for many years, the 1900s saw a change in society that defined the role of women. While many women in the urban centers of the East had severe restrictions placed on them by society, the situation in the rural West was quite different. Western women still had responsibilities outside the home and were responsible for feeding or otherwise taking care of their family's needs. As part of these responsibilities the women of the West not only were familiar with firearms, but also were often quite capable in their use.

Those women who attained fame for the use of firearms were definitely the exception. Often from the eastern half of the United States, these women were seen as examples of proper womanhood with the added dimension of excitement created by the association with firearms. This association, expected only from men—and upper class men, at that—was a definite draw on the east coast and was greatly exploited by the many "Wild West" shows. While the performers were feminine in appearance and dress, their skill with firearms and ability to showcase this skill set them apart from the rest of their gender and drew the crowds.

This attraction is only part of the story behind the success of the Topperweins. Adolph Topperwein, Ad for short, started as a demonstrator of Winchester firearms and ammunition. He traveled the country, showcasing the company's wares. As with most company representatives, Ad spent a lot of time visiting the Winchester headquarters in New Haven, Connecticut. It was on one of these trips that Ad and Elizabeth had the conversation that led to their marriage.

The married Topperweins toured for Winchester—with Ad performing and Elizabeth watching the shows and the admiring crowds. It didn't take Elizabeth long to tire of watching. She approached Ad one day and told him that she wanted to learn to shoot. He taught her and quickly discovered that she had a natural talent. After breaking 967 of 1,000 clay targets at the 1904 St. Louis Exposition, Winchester made her an official part of the show. This performance was a record for women and was better than most men could shoot. Within a couple of years, she was a draw in her own right. It was during this time that she gained the nickname Plinky, a name that conjures images of her "plinking" at targets. The name Plinky began to be used on posters and in newspaper reports, eventually finding its way into books and becoming so pervasive that it is difficult to find reference material that uses her given name.

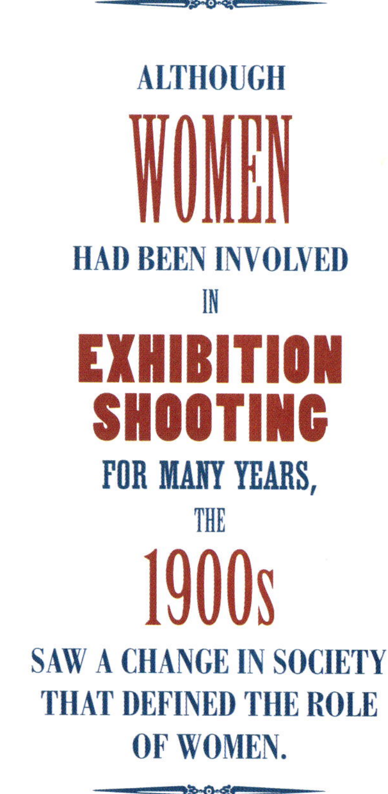

During her career, Plinky broke many more records—for men or women. Possibly her most important exhibition involved shooting 1,952 of 2,000 clay targets. She performed this task with a Winchester Model 97 slide-action shotgun over the course of five hours. With a rifle or with a shotgun, this latter-day Annie Oakley was the match of anyone she met. Annie Oakley, herself, even told Plinky that she was the greatest shooter of all time. Her skills with a shotgun led her to be one of only two women inducted into the Trapshooting Hall of Fame in 1969, its inaugural year. The other woman? Annie Oakley.

Plinky and Ad continued to work for Winchester until 1940. During this time, they helped to support the company and even trained the next generations of exhibition shooters, including Ernie and Dorothy Lind, and Herb Parsons, the "Showman Shooter" who worked for Winchester and Western Ammunition during the 1930s, '40s, and '50s. While Ad and Plinky were still performing, many hundreds (and even thousands) of people would regularly show up to see the Topperweins perform. Many would specifically show up to watch Plinky as she followed in the footsteps of Annie Oakley and other female shooters.

Winchester Model 1895 Rifle given to Zane Grey
by Winchester Repeating Arms Company

WRITING THE WEST

ZANE GREY

For well over two centuries, the mythological West has been defined and developed through the use of the pen. From the first reports of the people and animals of the Great Plains, there was a sense of disbelief regarding the land in the west of the fledgling nation. The later understanding of the region and what it meant was formed not as much by those who lived, explored, and worked in the West of the 1800s. More often, those who had barely traveled the West, if at all, wrote the stories. While the tales by inexperienced authors were historically and factually inaccurate, they were often easier to believe than the stories told by those who had lived the adventure and experienced the Wild West. The fiction was generally an easier read, something that has carried on to today.

As an example of this inability to believe factual representations, the region now known as Yellowstone National Park was the focus of many scoffed-at stories. John Colter, a member of Lewis and Clark's Corps of Discovery, an explorer and trapper, wrote a description of this region and its many geological wonders after a series of travels in the area. The facts of his journal were dismissed by many readers as being too fanciful to be true. It was only after William Clark voiced his support of Colter's descriptions that people began to accept it as factual. Later government-sponsored explorations received a similar response until accompanied by painters and photographers in order to visually document the features that, until then, were considered to be the products of creative writing.

Winchester Model 1895 Rifle given to Zane Grey by Winchester Repeating Arms Company

The truly creative writers were individuals like Ned Buntline, an early writer of the Western novels commonly called "dime novels." The stories that were told by many of these authors had strong heroes, often based on real people, performing fantastic shooting feats while rescuing the town, family or love interest from the bad guy. The bad guy could be a bank robber, cattle rustler, Indian, or wild animal. One story from Denmark even went so far as to have Buffalo Bill fighting ogres. Buntline and others helped to create this mythical West based on creating fictional stories involving factual personalities.

As the period of the Wild West ended, the beginnings of what we now consider to be a pseudo-realistic Western novel made an appearance. Owen Wister's *The Virginian* appeared in 1902, becoming the standard for many years. Wister's effect on the Western novel continued through the 20th century as Zane Grey, Louis L'Amour, and Larry McMurtry, among others, continued to build the story of a romantic West. While this romanticism began to be tempered as authors strove for more realism, many readers still choose the style as a way to escape to a simpler period of our history.

Zane Grey's role in this transformation was to improve the realism and language with more than 100 books, articles, and other writings that captured the attention of many boys and men who wanted to live the simpler life of the cowboy. Most of these writings ended up finding themselves on both the big screen and the little screen as they were adapted to film or television. While Grey did not live a life typical of those in his novels or during the time period represented in his books, he did live in the West and enjoyed a lifestyle that was "Western." One aspect of this lifestyle was his sporting activities. Both a hunter and an angler, Grey spent time outdoors pursuing these interests.

One of the rifles he owned, but most likely did not use for hunting, was the Winchester Model 1895 Rifle shown here. This rifle was a gift to Zane Grey from the Winchester Repeating Arms Company on February 28, 1924. Besides a semi-standard Winchester factory engraving, Grey's initials are in a stylized pattern replicated on the accompanying scabbard. An interesting aspect of the engraving is the use of copper in the bear design. The use of this common metal is strange in that most engravers will only ever use precious metals such as gold or silver. While there is gold present, the use of copper to create the ground under the bear is enough of an oddity to mention for its own sake.

This rifle, manufactured after the end of the "Wild West", and the man who owned it, writing about an era and lifestyle that was strange to him, both represent aspects of how the West was interpreted in the early 20th century. This semi-realistic view of the West would later taken to romantic extremes by Hollywood. Add a shiny rifle, dressed up to the point that it would never be a serious hunting weapon, and this description typifies the way in which the West is still seen by those who wish to live a civilized Western existence: choosing to believe the fiction rather than the fact.

FROM COWBOY TO ACTOR

GARY COOPER

Stagecoach, Winchester '73, High Noon, High Plains Drifter, The Sackets, Centennial, Gunsmoke, Bonanza, and others are classic movies and television productions about the West. These representations of the West, along with newer ones like *Silverado* and *Open Range* all show variations of a period and place that exists primarily in the viewer's mind. The industry that made these graphic representations has depended on the interest of the fan base, the quality of the story, and the skill of the actors. While the fan base is normally static and not much of the story is known before the film starts to roll, the acting talent can greatly affect the success. The films that are still considered classics were able to harness the energy of all three elements, creating a product that is still popular today.

Of the many stars of Western film, it is the men who often stand out in the minds of fans. John Wayne, Clint Eastwood, Gary Cooper, Jimmy Stewart, Michael Landon, Sam Elliot, the Carradines, and Tom Selleck are but a few of the many stars of the past seventy-five years' worth of Westerns. Oddly, most of these actors were not familiar with the West. A few of the successful Western actors, however, grew up in the region. Able to earn initial roles based on their skills and knowledge, these actors got their foot in the door in Hollywood. One of these actors, Gary Cooper, went this route, turning his Montana ranch experience into one of the most successful careers in film.

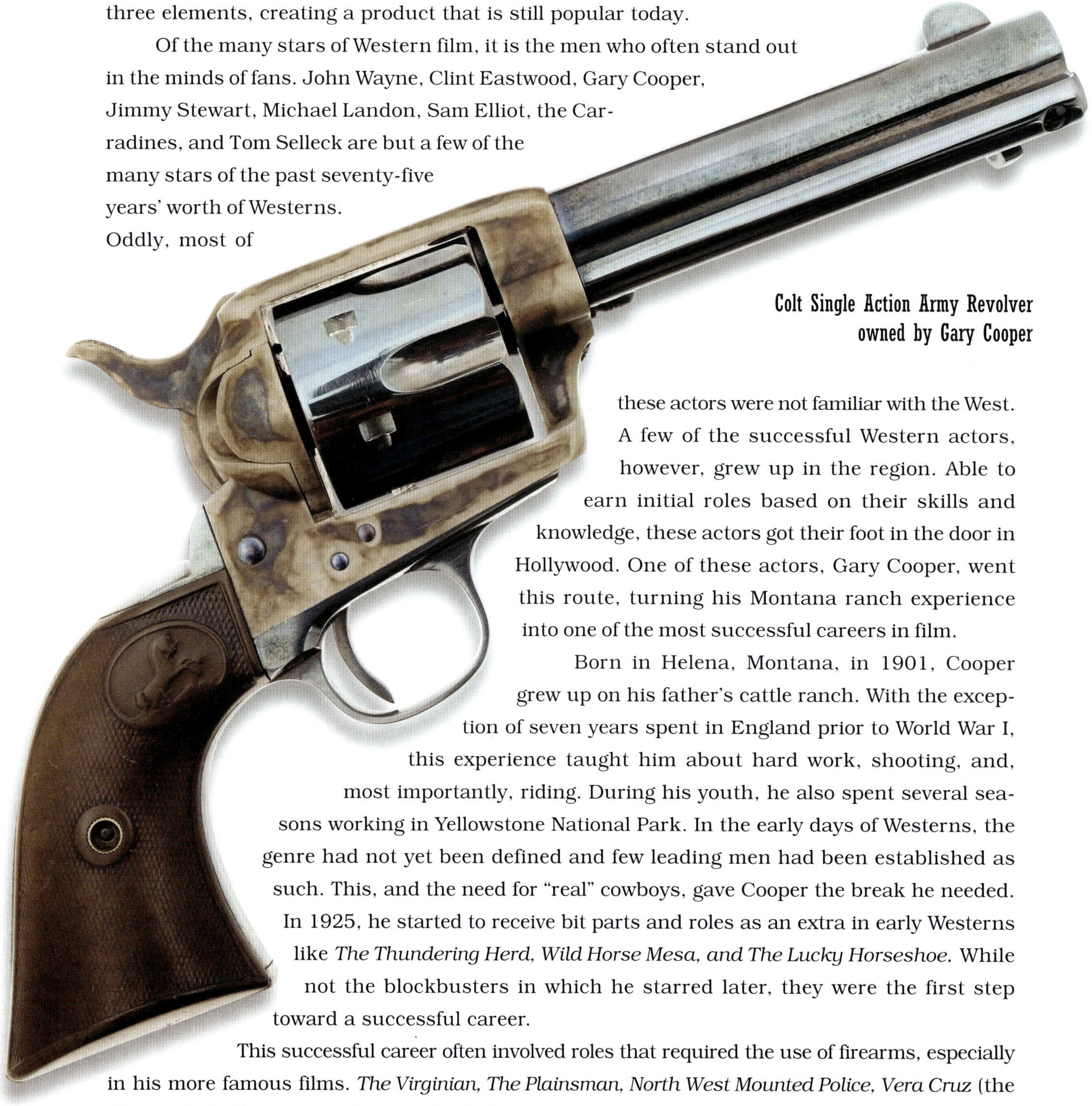

Colt Single Action Army Revolver owned by Gary Cooper

Born in Helena, Montana, in 1901, Cooper grew up on his father's cattle ranch. With the exception of seven years spent in England prior to World War I, this experience taught him about hard work, shooting, and, most importantly, riding. During his youth, he also spent several seasons working in Yellowstone National Park. In the early days of Westerns, the genre had not yet been defined and few leading men had been established as such. This, and the need for "real" cowboys, gave Cooper the break he needed. In 1925, he started to receive bit parts and roles as an extra in early Westerns like *The Thundering Herd, Wild Horse Mesa, and The Lucky Horseshoe.* While not the blockbusters in which he starred later, they were the first step toward a successful career.

This successful career often involved roles that required the use of firearms, especially in his more famous films. *The Virginian, The Plainsman, North West Mounted Police, Vera Cruz* (the film in which Cooper used the Colt Single Action Army revolver seen here) and other Westerns of his early films were interspersed with starring roles outside the genre. Besides straight entertainment like *Beau Geste* and *Mr. Deeds Goes to Town*, he also added biographical films like *Sergeant York* and *The Pride of the Yankees* to his resume. These films made Cooper a tidy fortune as he became, for a short while, one of the highest paid actors in the industry, making almost $500,000 in 1939.

Over the thirty-five years of Cooper's time in film, he was recognized by the Academy several times. His role as Sergeant Alvin York, a skilled marksman and Medal of Honor recipient from World War I, earned him the first of his Oscars. The second came for what was probably his most famous role, that of Marshal Will Kane in *High Noon*, This 1952 film about a lawman and the town he protected came to a head with the archetypal Western film plot device: the showdown on the main street of the town. This film affected the genre greatly as, previously, most Westerns tended to be rather formulaic. The dark view of the West seen in *High Noon* led to more Westerns of the style, presenting the West in a light that was not the celebratory, fantasy-based view used previously. Cooper's life came to a sad end in 1961 as he lost a fight with cancer—an end endured by many Western stars of his generation. It was during the last months of his life that Cooper received a final award from the Academy—a lifetime achievement award accepted in his stead by his friend, Jimmy Stewart.

Cooper always seemed natural in his roles. One reason for that was because so many of those characters were relatively similar to his own personality and beliefs. The solid performances in so many films led to his personal success. Quality performances helped many other actors in their own careers, when long-term success often depended on the health of the industry. While there have been lulls resulting from either a lack of audience interest or story quality, there has been a resurgence in both the number and quality of Westerns produced recently. This has led to productions like *Last Stand at Saber River* with Tom Selleck and even the 2003 television series *Firefly*, a Western occurring five hundred years in the future. As long as there is an interest in our history and that the films and television shows are of sufficient quality, we will have Westerns.

THE "SHOWMAN SHOOTER" BEHIND THE SCENES

HERB PARSONS

Sometimes the most famous guns of the West are the ones upon which movies are based. The film *"Winchester '73"* (Universal Studios, 1950) is one of these films. The gun upon which it was based, a "1 of 1000" Winchester Model 1873, is one of the rarest firearms in existence. Of the 720,610 1873s manufactured, only 136 of them were "1 of 1000s." Winchester used this film as part of a large advertising campaign, as the company located as many "1 of 1000s" as they could and toured these guns around the country as publicity for the movie. This publicity went into the history of the gun itself, explaining its origins and some of the folklore.

As with modern firearms, the manufacturers of the late 1800s test fired each gun produced by their company. During the testing of the 1873, the tester fired ten shots at a target. If the ten shots formed a small enough group, the rifle was sent back to be refitted with better wood, sights, and trigger. The rifle would then qualify as a "1 of 1000" (and receive a hefty increase in price from $40 to $100). The folklore that surrounds the "1 of 1000s" was enough to spur the production of the movie around one such rifle and the owner's search for it after it was stolen. This movie, filmed 75 years after the Model 1873 was introduced, was one of the better interpretations of the West, barring some flights of fancy.

A key scene at the beginning of the film involves a shooting competition with a "1 of 1000" as the prize. In this scene, there are shots of Jimmy Stewart shooting bullets through the center of a washer—proven with the use of a piece of tape. Most jaded moviegoers would claim that these shots were all faked and that Jimmy Stewart would not be able to perform such a stunt. These jaded moviegoers would be right—to a point. In the scene, the cameras follow the contest judge, the washer, and Jimmy Stewart simultaneously throughout the throwing and shooting. Although the same trick could be performed using trick photography or creative editing, the shooting was real and the target was hit. However, Stewart was using blanks.

What the camera did not show was a man in his early forties, wearing a red vest and ball cap, and carrying his rifle like a pro. This man, a true professional in every sense of the word, was Herb Parsons. Using the Winchester Model 71 seen here, Herb repeatedly put .351 caliber holes in everything thrown for him. Although washers were used for the scene, Universal Studios produced a large number of tokens emblazoned with the words "Universal Studios Pictures."

Winchester Model 71 Rifle used by Herb Parsons during the filming of **Winchester '73**

Winchester Model 71 Rifle used by Herb Parsons during the filming of **Winchester '73**

HERB REPEATEDLY PUT .351 CALIBER HOLES IN EVERYTHING THROWN FOR HIM.

These tokens were used as promotional items – after Herb shot them out of the air. One of these tokens is seen inlet into the stock. Surrounding this disk are the wood-burned autographs of the major stars of the film, among them Stewart, Dan Duryea, and Shelley Winters.

Parsons was one of the great demonstration shooters of all time. Following in the footsteps of Doc Carver, Annie Oakley, and the Topperweins, Parsons was the "Showman Shooter" of the mid-20th Century. He traveled the country from his home in Tennessee as an exhibition shooter for Winchester Firearms and Western Ammunition. As a professional descendent of the trick shots of the various "Wild West" shows, he was able to entertain and amaze with his running chatter and incredible speed and accuracy with rifles or shotguns. Many of his tricks were performed with the lever-action and slide-action descendants of Winchester's guns of the 19th Century.

Parson's abilities with firearms definitely qualified him to shoot on the set of *Winchester '73.* His participation in this film not only tied a product to an advertising medium, but it also tied the modern exhibition shooter to the trick shot artist of the late 1800s. Parson's use of a "modern" Model 71 did connect the production to the rough time period of the film. While the Model 71 was not descended from the Model 1873, it was a descendant of the Model 1886, the first true, large caliber Winchester rifle.

PART
VII

THE
CHANGING
AND
NEW
WEST

A Variety of "Suicide Specials" surrounding a gift to Cassie Le Fay-McGahn

ONLY GOOD FOR ONE THING . . .

SUICIDE SPECIALS

The classic view of the gun owner in the West is the grizzled sheriff or the no-good bandit armed with a large-caliber six-shooter. However, the use of guns in the West (and in America as a whole), was much more wide-spread and varied than the simple view shown in most popular stories. A large number of people–railroad workers, bankers, storeowners, women of various classes, and many city dwellers–owned small firearms for self defense. One of the most common firearms owned and carried by many Americans was a class of small, concealable revolvers that, while not as fear-inspiring as their larger cousins, could be used by many to protect themselves in many situations. Diminutive as they may be, the "Suicide Specials," as they came to be known, were possibly the most widely used handguns in the West.

These firearms, often chambered in a variety of small calibers (typically .22-.32 caliber), were little more than popguns when compared to the more famous Colts and Smith & Wessons in .44 and .45 caliber. The usefulness of these firearms may be suspect, but when the quality of 19th century medical care is taken into account, these firearms could be just as deadly as their larger brethren. Unfortunately for the recipient of the bullet, death from the infection caused by a .22 or .32 would take a longer time and be more painful than the normally quick death caused by a .44 or .45.

The first pistol of this type, the Smith & Wesson Number 1 Revolver, was the first true cartridge revolver. By drilling the chambers all of the way through the cylinder, shooters were able to step away from using loose black powder and lead balls. The ability to use metallic cartridges made the revolver easier to load, more dependable, and safer to use. Although the Number 1 was small, equivalent to the modern .22 Short, the industry and the public both saw the obvious benefits. Smith & Wesson continued to develop the idea with the Number 1 ½ and Number 2, both using larger cartridges. The Number 2, chambered for a .32 caliber rimfire cartridge was a favorite backup arm for many cavalry officers of the American Civil War.

Smith & Wesson had the market cornered on this type of firearm until 1872. When the patent expired on their use of the drilled-through cylinder, competition went in two distinct directions regarding the design. The Colt Single Action Army is an example of one of these directions—creating a new design for a large caliber revolver around the use of the previously patented cylinder. The other direction was the cheapest and easiest: copy the work done by others. Harrington & Richardson, Hopkins & Allen, Forehand & Wadsworth, Iver Johnson and many others initially made copies of the earlier Smith & Wessons, oftentimes making exact duplicates.

DIMINUTIVE AS THEY MAY BE, THE "SUICIDE SPECIALS," AS THEY CAME TO BE KNOWN, WERE POSSIBLY THE MOST WIDELY USED HANDGUNS IN THE WEST.

These duplicates were inexpensive, often sold to dealers for $5 to $10 per dozen. Being readily available, inexpensive, and easily concealable, they became very common in the urban areas of the country. Businessmen, tradesmen, politicians, police officers, and prostitutes owned them. By the 20th century, medicine had reached a point at which the wounds from these arms were not normally fatal. The term "Suicide Specials," came to be used in the 1900s as a result of the only presumed and effective purpose for using such firearms.

The centerpiece of the small collection shown at the beginning of this chapter is a 20th century gift to a prostitute. It is a .32 rimfire Hopkins & Allen XL3 revolver that has been modified by applying a gold wash and replacing the original plastic or rubber grips with grips made of mother-of-pearl. The personalization goes even further with the inscription in the grip. The grip on the left side reads, "To my friend Cassie" while the right side reads, "Every inch a lady." On the surface this appears to be a simple gift to a woman named Cassie.

The story goes much deeper than that, however. The Cassie named on the gun was Cassie Le Fay-McGahn, for many years the Madam of a "sporting house" in Cody, Wyoming. While Cassie's House was in business from 1910 to 1955, she befriended many prominent businessmen and politicians in both the town and the state. While there are some guesses as to the name of the individual who gave the pistol to Cassie, the name is apparently only known to a few. It is also unknown if Cassie regularly carried the pistol or even fired it. It is, however, an interesting means by which to examine the life of a Western town in the 20th century, a town in which the "Wild West" still seemed to be alive.

A GREAT DESIGNER, A GIRL, AND A GUN

THE WINCHESTER MODEL 1894

One of the most influential firearms of the settled West, the Winchester Model 1894, became a jack-of-all-trades of the American West. It was used for hunting, for defense, and for simply hanging on the wall. It was a gun that almost everyone could afford. Additionally, with no design changes over the hundred-plus years of its history, it is probably the most durable American product ever made. Telling three stories, this particular Model 1894 can demonstrate firearms, social, and hunting history.

John Moses Browning, America's foremost and most prolific arms designer, was the creative genius behind this firearm. Browning, born and raised in Ogden, Utah, worked as a designer for many of the major manufacturers. Many of his designs were ground breaking and a number are still in production at this writing. Besides a number of smaller companies in the United States and Italy manufacturing reproductions of his work, a few of Browning's designs are still manufactured under the original names. His designs for Winchester included virtually every gun manufactured from 1885 to 1902. The Models of 1885, 1886, 1892, 1894, 1895, 1897, and others were directly from or influenced by his designs.

ONE OF THE KEYS TO THE SUCCESS OF THE MODEL 1894 IS THE PRIMARY CARTRIDGE USED IN THIS RIFLE.

His design for a semiautomatic pistol led to the Colt Model 1900, a design that eventually became the Model 1911, and other, smaller-caliber pistols. Colt's Manufacturing Company still manufactures the Model 1911 semiautomatic pistol, one of the most copied pistol designs in firearms history. Browning later took an improved version of this design to the Belgian firm of Fabrique Nationale. The current incarnation of Fabrique Nationale, FN Herstal, still manufactures a modern version of the Hi-Power pistol they started to produce in 1935. Browning's other inventions in firearms may not have had much of an effect on the West, but they did affect the rest of the world. The Browning Machine Gun and the Browning Automatic Rifle were two of the most influential military designs of the 20th century. A modified version of his machine gun is still in use by more militaries than any other heavy machine gun.

Winchester has manufactured the 1894 for over a century. During this period, over five million 1894s have come off of the assembly line with virtually no internal modifications from

Winchester Model 1894 Rifle owned by Irma Cody Garlow, daughter of "Buffalo Bill" Cody

the first rifle made. One of the keys to the success of the Model 1894 is the primary cartridge used in this rifle. The .30 Winchester Center Fire—more commonly known as the .30-30—is considered by many to be a classic deer cartridge. The designation .30-30 derives from the use of a .30 caliber bullet and a propellant charge equivalent to 30 grains (by weight) of smokeless powder—not 30 grains (by volume) of black powder, as many people think. This cartridge has been cited by some as killing more deer than any other round, even the .30-06. The reasons behind this include the low price of ammunition and the ability of this round to stop deer-sized game. While the range of this cartridge is not competitive with those used for many of the larger big game animals, this did nothing to prevent its use in heavily wooded areas across the country. The sturdy nature of this firearm and the small size of the carbine model also allowed it to be packed in a scabbard attached to the saddle easier and safer than any scoped rifle.

One of the people who chose a Model 1894 as a hunting rifle was Irma Cody, the youngest daughter of Bill and Louisa Cody. Born in 1883, the same year as Buffalo Bill's Wild West first tour, Irma literally grew up around the show and the trappings of Bill Cody's lifestyle. As a result of her father's support of women's equality, she learned to ride and shoot and become an independent woman in a manner that would not become standard for at least several more decades. In 1902, following his development of the town of Cody, Wyoming, Bill Cody opened a luxury hotel in the town. He named this hotel after Irma. With the proximity to outstanding hunting areas, Irma went hunting in the area of Cody and Yellowstone National Park with this 1894. While hunting is still considered by many to be a "man's sport", women have always hunted and Irma was no different.

In 1908 Irma married Fred Garlow, a lawyer who worked for Bill Cody. Within several years, Fred and Irma had a daughter and two sons, Jane, Fred, and Bill. Unfortunately the children were orphaned during of the influenza outbreak of 1917.

Of the children, Bill Cody Garlow was the only one to seek the fame attained by his grandfather. While he did become a spokesman for Daisy BB Guns and toured as "Buffalo Bill," little else came of the name. The descendents of Bill Cody are still involved in the story of Buffalo Bill and the town he created, though, helping to make sure the stories and the histories are accurate and that new generations continue to learn about the West.

The relationship of women, firearms, the West, and a gun designer from Utah may seem tenuous at first, but the connections are there when examined. These stories, when put together, help to tell the story of the West in a different light than normal. As a result of three decades of repeating arms designs from Winchester, a gundesigner from the West was able to make a firearm that has become one of the most popular guns in history. Many hunters, men, women, and children used it. The users were not just the typical hunter, but also the privileged that wanted the best gun for the job. A classic in every sense of the word, the Model 1894 is an American legend.

MARKETING FOR THE NEW WEST

A SAVAGE MODEL 1899

Change is a constant, though there was a period during which change seemingly slowed in the West. During the first part of the 20th century, the West appeared to settle down. The major train routes had been established, mines were up and running, all of the cattle had made the trip to the various ranches, and the towns and cities had not seen the diaspora that would occur during and after World War II. The West was settled and the region's inhabitants began to adopt the trappings of those who lived elsewhere around the country, though they practiced activities that were associated with the West. Among these activities was hunting of different types. As a result of the various technological advances, hunters were able to enjoy a variety of arms and ammunition that was specialized beyond anything seen previously.

Before the development of smokeless powder at the end of the 19th century, longarms were limited in their capabilities and versatility. This led to most guns being easy to use at short range, but at ranges beyond 100 to 200 yards, a level of skill and training was necessary. Hunting rifles were generally .40 caliber or larger. Target rifles were in the .25 to .38 caliber range and .22 caliber firearms were generally used for shooting galleries and small game. Part of the division of these calibers was the result of the use of black powder.

The effectiveness of the black powder guns relied on the size of bullet that could be used and the amount of powder that could fit in the casing. If a shooter wanted to make a particular cartridge more powerful, he would need to lengthen or widen the case. With smokeless powder, this changed. Different types of smokeless powder could give noticeable increases in pressure, propelling bullets farther and faster than seen before. As an additional benefit, smokeless powder burns relatively cleanly, meaning that the residue left in the barrel does not build up in the manner of black powder. This allowed very powerful, small caliber arms to be feasible.

Lastly, using the same frame for a variety of interchangeable barrels became a much easier task.

With the advent of smokeless powder, the standards concerning which caliber to use for a specific task changed drastically. All types of shooting saw new calibers excel as designers and ammunition companies introduced literally hundreds of new cartridges. While many of these rounds were dismissed within a few years, a small number have lasted through the twentieth century. A short list will include a large number of .30 caliber cartridges used by the world's militaries and a number of high-powered cartridges for the semi-automatic handguns developed at the turn of the century. While a few black powder era cartridges have remained, most have disappeared.

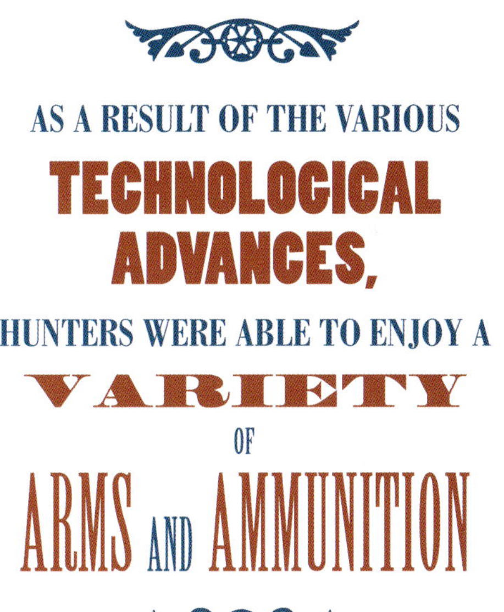

One of the cartridges that was a "hit and miss", so to speak, was the .22 Savage High-Power. The ammunition designer Charles Newton created this cartridge by modifying a .25-35 cartridge case to accept a .22 caliber bullet. In this manner, it is an example of how ammunition designers attempt to improve a cartridge by changing the size of bullet used. Although this cartridge was successful at the time as a small-game and target cartridge, it did have its drawbacks. Despite company advertisements citing its ability to be used for lion, tiger, and even elephant, it was sometimes unable to successfully take American big game animals. Competition did not

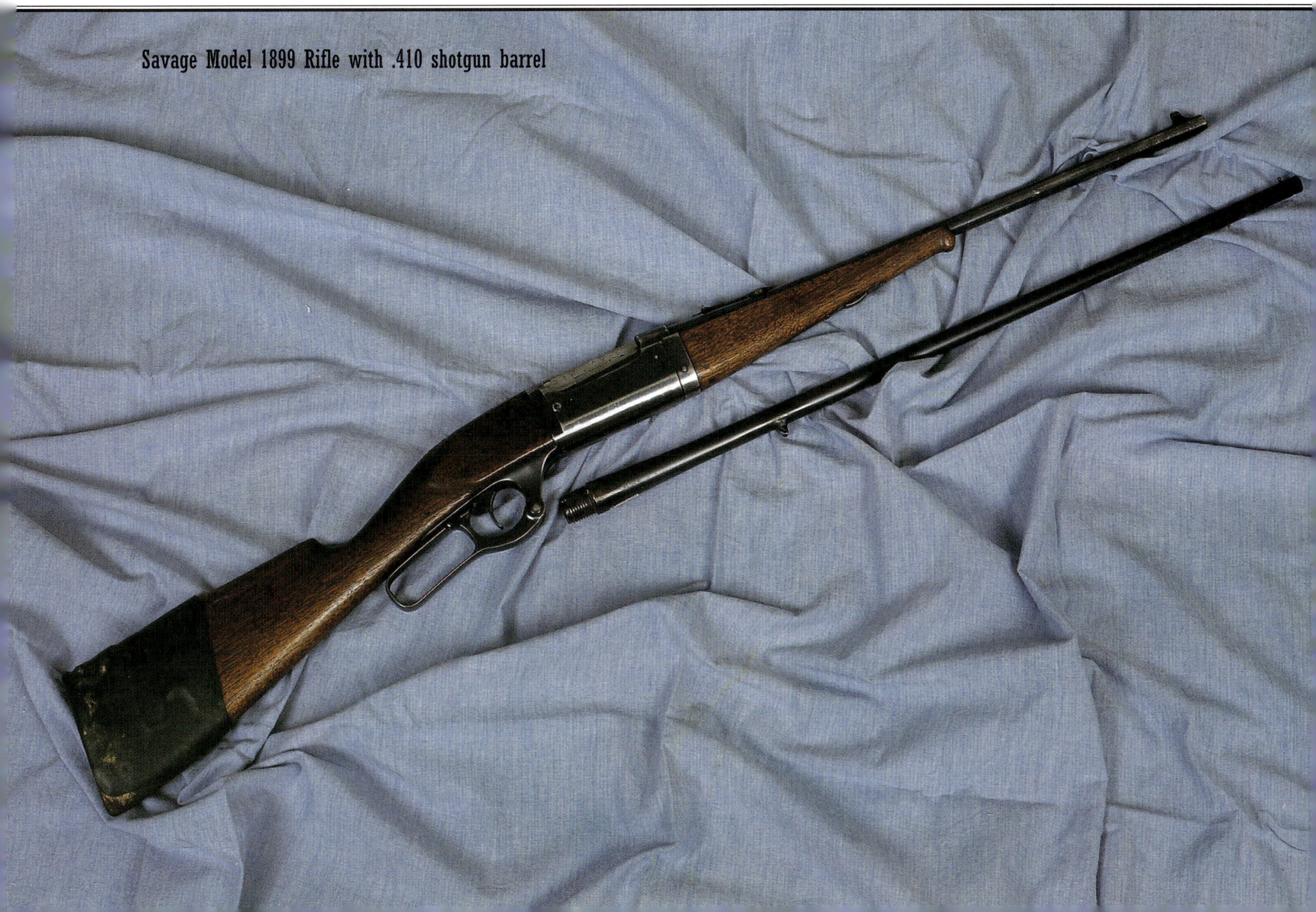

Savage Model 1899 Rifle with .410 shotgun barrel

help matters as similar, but much better, ammunition introduced by Winchester and Remington took over the market niche that Savage had filled.

As an example of a successful cartridge, Savage followed up the introduction of the .22 High-Power with a .25 caliber cartridge, also Newton-designed. This cartridge was, in contrast to the High-Power, a long-term success. The .250-3000, as it came to be called, was everything the High-Power and other cartridges hoped to be: accurate, with little recoil, and strong enough to be used on any game up to deer. The name, a marketing ploy, was based on the cartridge's velocity—a .25 caliber bullet propelled at 3000 feet per second. Until this cartridge, many shooters considered this velocity unattainable. This cartridge proved them wrong and is still in production.

The gun used by Savage for these cartridges and others was the Model 1899, later called the Model 99, manufactured by Savage for almost a century. Basically an improved Model 1895, the 99 had a rotary magazine, complete with a counter that let the shooter know, with a glance, how much ammunition was left in the magazine. The lever action allowed fast operation and the ejection of the cartridges were to the right of the shooter, not straight up, as with the Winchester lever guns. This allowed the mounting of a scope; something that greatly aided the use of the powerful cartridges used by Savage, but could prevent proper operation of the Winchesters.

An additional feature of the Model 99 was an available .410 shotgun barrel that could be used in place of the standard rifle barrel. With this, the owner could use the same rifle for deer and for game birds. Hunters appreciated the versatility of such a gun as a way to save money while filling the cooking pot in an economical manner. Another benefit of this was the ability to protect livestock from small predators during the non-hunting portion of the year.

A classic of the smokeless powder era, the Savage Model 99 was an example of how modern manufacturing and design techniques, smokeless powder, and American ingenuity could produce high-quality firearms for the civilian trade. Guns like this and the ammunition that was used in them helped to support much of the rural West in the "settling down" period of the early 20th century. As the inhabitants tried to redefine themselves, the ability to procure their own food and live the life of those who came before them helped to establish an identity that was based on, but different from, that of their predecessors.

A STRANGE FIND FROM THE PAST

THE "CHICKEN COOP" GUN

Living in the West was not always an easy task. When the animals agreed with you, the weather could be too rainy or too dry. If the amount of rain was just right, wind could destroy all around you. If the weather was perfect, the people could probably be expected to cause a problem.

Marlin Model 1893 rifle with ranch-mounted .410 shotgun barrel

If everything else seemed to be all right, then there were the inevitable supply issues that came from living several hundred to several thousand miles away from the nearest railhead. It is no surprise that one of the attributes given to the citizens of the West is ingenuity.

Interesting problems required creative solutions—especially when the equipment at hand became broken or otherwise unusable. Parts from one piece of machinery were used to repair other machines. Wire from a fence may have been used to tie down loose objects, or vice versa. If something was broken, the good parts would be saved and used in a different project later.

Sometime in the 1920s or 1930s, a Marlin Model 1893 carbine became a useless hunk of metal. It is not known how, but this Marlin, serial number 246784, was rendered unusable. Chances are that the barrel was bent in an accident. Alternatively, the barrel may have been plugged with mud or snow, causing it to bulge or burst when fired. Regardless of the cause, the original .38-55 carbine barrel is no longer on this firearm.

The real surprise with this firearm is the current barrel. While there is the expectation that one would replace the barrel with another rifle or carbine barrel, this did not happen. The replacement barrel is not from Marlin. It is not even a rifled barrel, much less a .38 caliber barrel. The new barrel is a .410 smoothbore. Taken from an unknown .410 gauge shotgun, the barrel is probably the remains of a shotgun that, most likely, shared the same fate as the carbine. Perhaps the stock split or broke. Maybe the action on the single-barrel, break-action shotgun became damaged or otherwise unusable. Whatever happened, the barrel was saved for future use. That use was the creation of a new gun.

The "Franken-gun" that came out of this odd combination was what might be expected, a lever-action that isn't really a lever-action and a shotgun that isn't really a shotgun. The shotgun barrel was screwed into the receiver and tack-welded into place. While the lever still works, the loading gate is too small for even the smallest .410 gauge shot shells. Accordingly, working the lever will not load a cartridge, but it will open the action, allowing you to insert or extract a cartridge.

The telling point of this firearm is the location in which it was found—an old chicken coop on an abandoned ranch. It was found leaning in a corner, the best spot for an old gun that was probably used to shoot at chicken hawks, foxes, skunks, or raccoons. As for why it was left in the coop, there could be any number of reasons. Unless they were expecting to be attacked by any number of enemies, on two legs or four, most people simply did not carry guns regularly–and usually not while gathering eggs. And a gun of this type was not good for much more than the uses cited above. While the shotgun was probably the most common firearm used in the West, the .410 was just too light to be used for shooting anything bigger than small game and varmints. With the leftovers of two old guns, this creative combination was probably seen as a disposable, albeit useful, commodity.

Probably left by its last owner, who either passed on or moved on, the gun was found by a later generation that bought the ranch. Continuing the tradition of the rural West, the original land owner was taking care of business the only way he knew how—take care of the land and the land will take care of you. And when all else fails, modify your tools and how you use them in order to meet the situation. The changes in life were met in a straight-forward manner and using any weapon in the farmer's arsenal—figuratively and literally. In this case, the best tool for a job was a gun cobbled together from the castoffs of two others. Sometimes the best solution for a problem is the most creative solution.

THE WEST REVISITED

A RUGER SUPER BLACKHAWK

When interpreting the "Wild West," it is important to study the period, its people, objects, and events. But without looking at the historiography of the paradigm and the later interpretations, both academic and popular, a complete understanding of the period is unattainable. To use a firearms-related example, the tendency of most popular representations of the "Wild West" has been to display Colt and Winchester as the only guns in great use. This representation continues further through the selection of the costume elements shown, specifically the pistol belt with holster and any other accoutrements to help support the fantasy image of The West.

This fantasy began with the early black-and-white movies and serializations of the 1940s and '50s, and continued through to the various television series of the 1960s and '70s. It became "The West" as understood by those who saw the stories represented, believing that the fantasy on the screen was as true as any history book discussing the era. Sidestepping the "History vs. Hollywood" debate that could erupt from such a discussion, the representation of a cowboy was often as black-and-white as the film stock used in the production.

Discounting the ever-present faithful steed and adoring girlfriend, the "Cowboy" was left with the equipment strapped to his waist. This equipment varied from production to production and character to character, but it was always present. More important, this equipment was the viewer's first opportunity to make a determination as to the qualities of the character. As with all other first impressions, the initial presentation of a character and the costume laid the groundwork for later interpretation of the character and their actions. The tools examined here are the pistol belt, the revolver, and the knife (often replaced, however, with another revolver).

The pistol belt, besides being the means to carry equipment, was the first costume article that allowed the viewer to make interpretations. The condition and general appearance of the pistol belt could vary greatly. The unwritten messages presented in these differences could tell a number of stories about the owner. A well worn, but clean, pistol belt could identify someone as a professional cowboy with many miles under the saddle or, possibly, as a gunslinger who knows better than to bring attention to himself. On the other hand, a "pretty" pistol belt, brimming with shiny cartridges and shinier silver decoration could identify someone as a well-to-do person with more money than sense or, more often, a hero of the Hollywood definition, complete with white hat and shiny gun.

The gun itself, generally a Colt Peacemaker in modern representations, could tell stories as well. However, the physical appearance of the gun in popular entertainment can often say more about the artistic/historic value of the production than many other aspects of the costumes or set dressing.

Ruger Super Blackhawk with belt and knife given to the Vice President of the United States, Richard Cheney

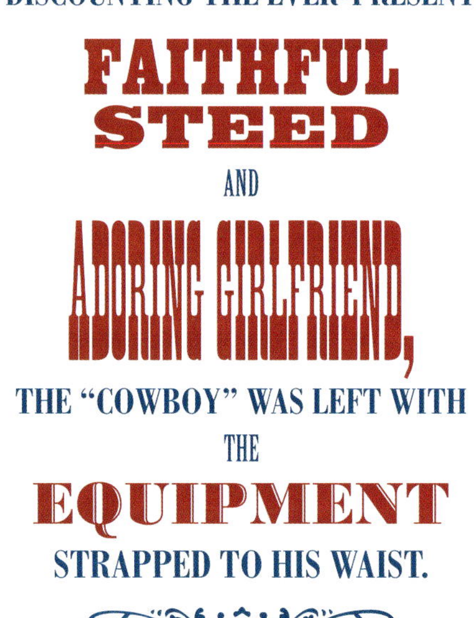

Identifying the make and model of the firearm can help the viewer determine if the movie takes place in a specific time period or simply during the generic period of the "Wild West." Any decoration of the firearm can help determine whether the gun is to be seen as a tool, in the case of a simple, blued firearm, or as a showpiece or other sign of position, in the case of a highly embellished and plated firearm.

The appearance of a knife can produce a variety of interpretations. The simplest inference is that the owner is prepared for any event—from defending himself to butchering an animal. The more complex explanation is that the owner is willing to kill with a knife, an act that can be seen as being much more personal than the distance afforded by using a gun. Again, the appearance of the knife is important in this determination—is the knife utilitarian in form or is it decorative?

Bringing many of these questions to the forefront is a recent gift to the Cody Firearms Museum. Consisting of a heavily tooled belt with holster and knife sheath, an engraved, but blued, revolver, and a large Bowie knife, this set represents each of the aforementioned costume elements. The belt, appropriately enough, was manufactured by the Hollywood firm of Alfonso's, a company known for many years as a supplier to the movie industry. The knife, one of the premier items in the catalog of knife company Cold Steel, is modified by the addition of an ornamental elk antler grip. The revolver is a Ruger Super Blackhawk with simple engraving and a dedication to the original recipient, who determined that Cody would be the best destination for the set.

While the appearance and composition of this set can be discussed and analyzed in many ways, the former owner of this rig will surely have his own ideas as to the meaning of the individual pieces. He has every right to do so. However, the meaning and intent of this particular gift to this particular individual (and a matching rig to his boss), achieves a new level of meaning upon the disclosure that he is none other than Vice President of the United States Richard Cheney.

MARKETING OUR HERITAGE

COMMEMORATIVE FIREARMS

During much of the recent past—at least for the past few hundred years—the celebration of a particular event has often received much attention, even after many years. Following the American Revolution and the American Civil War, commemorative prints were sold through national presses and by salesmen around the country. The 20th century saw more of the same as pictures, plates, glasses, and even alcoholic beverages and soft drinks were sold in an attempt to commemorate an event or anniversary—and often to simply make money under the pretense of patriotism or reverence. The firearms industry played into this game as well, selling many limited editions of their arms in order to commemorate various aspects of the history of the West. While the most active in this area was Winchester, each of the major arms companies and many smaller companies have entered commemorative arms into the field.

With Winchester's reorganization in 1963, the company embarked on a strategy to increase their sales while marketing their name on a wider scale. By choosing particular topics of the Old West, the company was able to sell their arms to individuals specifically interested in those topics. Attractive topics to Winchester were the Well Fargo Stage, the "Golden Spike" completing the Trans-continental railroad, and the Texas Rangers. Aditionally organizations could team up with Winchester to raise money through the sale of these arms. The Buffalo Bill Historical Center partnered with Winchester in this manner in order to raise funds to support new construction. The third reason to create a commemorative arm was to celebrate a company anniversary. Winchester did this for the 125th anniversary of the company. Marlin and Savage did the same as well in order to celebrate corporate anniversaries.

Winchester "Cowboy Commemorative", "Texas Ranger", and "Wells Fargo" commemorative carbines

Winchester "Cowboy Commemorative" and "Wells Fargo" commemorative carbines

Often sold in limited numbers, many commemorative firearms have held their financial value. The historical and celebratory value is what attracts many to these arms. From 1967 to 1970, Colt manufactured a series of 1911A1 pistols that honored four battles of World War I and the European and Pacific theaters of World War II. Many of the commemorative arms sold by Winchester were of this same sort, honoring different aspects of western history, from Annie Oakley to the Royal Canadian Mounted Police to John Wayne. With only a modest increase in the purchase price, anyone can usually afford to own one of these guns.

In a related vein, non-profit organizations often team up with manufacturers in order to raise funds. From the Boy Scouts of America to the Buffalo Bill Historical Society, organizations receive a portion of the sale price for each firearm sold. With this additional cost, the manufacturer often increases the purchase price a bit more. This amount is normally represented in print and rarely exceeds a few hundred dollars. The organization on the receiving end normally needs (and appreciates) this money and the gift it represents. The largest production run of any gun of this kind may well be the Winchester Model 94 Buffalo Bill Commemorative set of a rifle and carbine. With more than 112,000 produced between the two versions, over $1,000,000 was raised for the Buffalo Bill Historical Center.

In celebration of the corporate or technological history of firearms, many companies have produced special firearms to advertise the impact of their products on history. While companies normally use mechanical methods such as roll stamps and computer controlled bits to engrave many of the previously discussed commemoratives, companies have often relied on the

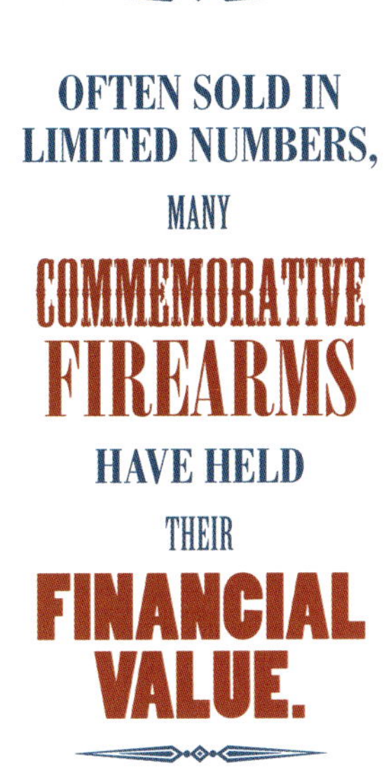

services of skilled engravers for guns celebrating their own past. These guns are often of two types. Some may be special points within a company's production while others represent anniversaries. Many companies select guns with serial numbers divisible by one hundred thousand, five hundred thousand, or even one million to engrave and use as product samples and sales tools. Just prior to this writing, the Marlin Firearms Company donated a highly engraved Model 336, the grandson of the Model 1893, to the National Shooting Sports Foundation. This rifle—serial number 4,000,000—was auctioned by the organization in order to raise money for the Hunting & Shooting Sports Heritage Fund. As an example of anniversary models, Winchester used the opportunity of their 125th Anniversary to make a limited edition of their Model 94. Sixty-One Model 94s produced that year (1991) with a serial number ending in 5000 or 10000 were highly engraved by hand. Italian engravers embellished these carbines, true works of art.

The last quarter century has seen an interesting twist to the concept of commemorative firearms. Several companies have begun to market what could best be called "concept commemoratives." These companies select "commemorative" (and occasionally questionable) themes and produce arms befitting the subject matter. While some of these arms are legitimate products of Colt, Winchester, and others, many of the guns used are reproduction or replica arms. The embellishment on these firearms normally consists of laser-engraving (an inexpensive and physically shallow form of engraving) and a metallic wash for detail points in the design. Generally sold through magazine advertisements, these arms often go for a surprisingly high price. While an increased price may be seen as a benefit for a particular individual or organization, most of these arms have no indication of a recipient of any proceeds. As for any opportunists looking to buy these arms as an investment, there is no sign of appreciation, much less a market for the resale of these arms.

Winchester "Cowboy Commemorative", "Texas Ranger", and "Wells Fargo" commemorative carbines

The subject of commemorative arms, as with much of the commemorative market, is a broad field. While many of these objects are sold in a legitimate manner, with the genuine hope that the purchaser will enjoy the product and celebrate the subject, some are certainly sold only in order to make money. Although this is not much different from earlier attempts to sell commemorative objects, it does sometimes cheapen the memory of the events and people involved in the subject. Regardless of the seller's motive, the buyer who chooses to celebrate the subject of the commemorative object–be it plate, print, or pistol–willingly pays the cost of a commemorative object.

PLAYING COWBOY

MODERN REPLICAS

After World War II, Western culture became a stereotyped vision of sequins and six-shooters. The popular understanding of the West, based in film and, later, television, was a caricature of the original. Gaudy shirts, shiny guns, and palomino horses became de rigueur for the heroes. A similar line of thinking led the villains to wear black from head to toe. The theatrics involved in the cinematic representation of the West have been seen by many historians to represent the polarized view of the nation during the 1940s and 1950s. This black-and-white view of the world—and of the West—changed in the 1960s and 1970s with the acceptance by many of much more diverse viewpoints. The heroes often resembled the villains of the previous generation in dress and action. As the world became more complicated, many Americans came to desire the supposedly simpler time of their youth or even earlier. This desire became reality in many methods. One of the methods chosen was to reenact what many Americans see as the epitome of a "simpler time"—The Wild West.

Although a number of American and European manufacturers have been making replica arms based on—in some cases identical to—the guns of the "Old West" since the 1950s, the market for many years was seen as a fringe area, as most gun buyers seemingly wanted newer designs for arms. In the handgun market, newer cartridges like the .357 and .44 magnums captured the attention of revolver shooters. Rifle buyers gravitated toward modern bolt-action and semiautomatic arms. Shotgun shooters also went toward the newer designs, in many cases eschewing the venerable side-by-side. With no sizeable interest in the guns of the West, this portion of the market floundered until popular culture began to focus on the period of the West as an interest for recreation and escapist fun.

Modern (3rd Generation) Colt Single Action Army Revolver

This interest breathed new life into the "cowboy gun" market in the 1980s as a number of individuals began to modify popular shooting sports of the day to embrace the use of single action revolvers, double-barrel shotguns, and lever action rifles. Where the previous competitions had been based in law enforcement or military scenarios involving hostages, holdups, and military attacks, the altered versions replicated stage robberies, showdowns at high noon, and the inevitable shootout at the OK Corral. These competitions, scored against the clock, became an instant hit as the new outdoor shooting sport of Cowboy Action Shooting was developed. With two large national organizations, the Single Action Shooting Society (SASS) and the National Congress of Old West Shootists (NCOWS), this sport is currently the fastest growing outdoors shooting sport.

With over 60,000 members the Single Action Shooting Society, founded in 1987, represents the largest group of these shooters. The rules established by SASS have defined the Cowboy Action Shooting in a number of ways. With safety as the first rule and fun as the second, many participants have taken the sport up as a hobby and favorite weekend activity. The effect of the Western enthusiasts desire to have fun while being serious is readily apparent. As the regulations require appropriate dress, as well as appropriate firearms, there is a cottage industry that supports the shooters by offering everything from boots to hats. In talking to some of the competitors, it becomes obvious that the shooting is sometimes secondary to the fun of adopting an alias and dressing the part. Thus many participants may spend nearly as much on their clothes and gear as they spend on their guns.

The guns required include two single action revolvers, one rifle, and one shotgun, with the rifle and shotgun required to be of a type common to the era. There are additional restrictions of caliber, operation, and authenticity. Additional guns may be required if the competitor

Navy Arms Model 1866 engraved as a gift to William Garlow Cody

chooses to participate in competitions involving long range shooting or the use of derringers. To supply this need, a number of firearm companies have introduced offerings in this area. Colt, Ruger, the US Firearms Company, and Winchester are only a few of the American companies making guns that regulations allow. Several Italian, Russian, and Asian companies manufacture similar guns for the same market. With the number and types of guns involved, competitors are looking at investing $1500 or more for the lower-priced, entry-level guns. Equipping oneself with higher-quality or antique arms can quickly raise the cost to several thousands of dollars.

One of the higher quality guns produced for this sport is the Colt Single Action Army Revolver. A modern version of the Colt Model 1873, the current Single Action Army is considered by the company and collectors as the "3rd generation" of production. With "1st generation" production ostensibly ending in 1940 and the "2nd generation" production lasting from 1956 to 1975, the revolvers currently being produced are considered by some collectors to be "replicas" of the originals. Regardless of the semantics involved in a discussion of this sort, the current Single Action Army is of the same quality, if not higher, as those produced over a century ago under the blue dome of the Colt Factory along the Connecticut River in Hartford. The revolver seen here was used in the exhibit "Colt: Legacy of a Legend" at the Buffalo Bill Historical Center in the summer of 2003. As an example of the current production, Colt gave this revolver and others to the Cody Firearms Museum following the exhibit. While finances prevent many Cowboy Action Shooting competitors from owning a true Colt Single Action Army, the guns many of them use are copies of the original.

As an example of other arms produced for this market, an embellished Navy Arms Model 1866 carbine comes to mind. Started in 1956 by Val Forgett, Sr., Navy Arms was one of the primary suppliers of replica firearms for many years. Navy Arms was, for many years, the primary source of arms and equipment that replicated the "Old West" and earlier periods of our company. To this day they are still one of the larger suppliers of such goods. This carbine, manufactured by the Italian company Uberti, was a gift from Val Forgett, Sr. to Bill Cody's grandson in 1966. As 1966 was the centennial of Winchester's introduction of their first production firearm, this carbine was intended to celebrate the history of a historic company. As is evident with the engraving, it is also intended to celebrate a famous American, William F. "Buffalo Bill" Cody.

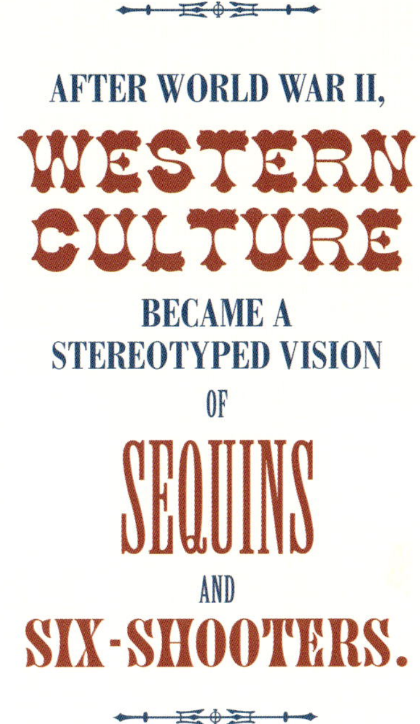

Many people underestimate the importance of the Wild West era in American history. If gauged only by the interest held in dressing up and playing cowboy, it is obvious that this era is still important. It is an area of interest that allows whole families to experience American history. Any celebration of the period does engender a discussion of the era and those who experienced it firsthand, allowing all of us to better appreciate both their time and ours.

Navy Arms Model 1866 engraved as a gift to William Garlow Cody

"YOU'LL SHOOT YOUR EYE OUT!"

MODERN AIR RIFLES

Among the memories of many American youths are imaginary games of "Cowboys and Indians," fighting the Germans or Japanese during World War II, or Davy Crockett defending the Alamo. Among the less violent imaginary adventures were the "great hunter" looking for bear or lion, and the jungle explorer looking for lost cities of gold. Never mind that these games may have taken place in the city park, a nearby creek bed, or simply on a hillside behind your best friend's house. These games played by youth were as varied as the parts of the country in which they lived, the time in which they grew up, or even the props they used to play-act their "roles." In addition, playing these games often actually taught skills and character traits not learned in today's computerized "adventures." Much of this play later helped these youth become better people who had a sense of responsibility, attention, and dedication.

The players in these make-believe dramas would have made a ragged army. Equipped with broken tree branches, yard sticks, broom handles, popguns, and, if lucky, a BB gun, motley militias such as this have defended many a neighborhood from marauding Indians,

Lukens Air Rifle and Girandoni Repeating Air Rifle paired with a Daisy

invading Nazis, and jungle pygmies, however fictional or politically incorrect the threat may be. Despite the well-founded warnings of, "You'll shoot your eye out!" many an American child grew up with a BB gun in their hands.

While the air rifle is centuries old, the variation known today as a BB gun is a relatively recent development. Before the turn of the 20th century, the air rifle was still an oddity—seeing use in carnival midways, indoor ranges, and other small venues. In the first part of the 20th century, companies began to develop inexpensive air rifles that were more readily affordable than even the .22 rifles produced by the likes of Winchester, Stevens, and Remington.

With the expansion of broadcast entertainment in the 20th century, starting with radio and later including movies and television, the ability to market goods to a national audience quickly made ripples in how products were advertised. Product tie-ins begin to be de rigueur in all of these media forms. From decoder rings to Ovaltine, the producers and advertising agencies found ways to support the entertainment while selling their varied products.

DESPITE THE WELL-FOUNDED WARNINGS OF, "YOU'LL SHOOT YOUR EYE OUT!" MANY AN AMERICAN CHILD GREW UP WITH A BB GUN IN THEIR HANDS.

The relevance of this situation to BB guns can be summed up in two words: Red Ryder. Named after a radio show based around a fictional hero of the Wild West, the Red Ryder soon found its way to the top of many Christmas lists. The fame of this gun lasted much longer than the radio show. It was even a featured prop in the film *A Christmas Story* (MGM, 1983), the story of a family's Christmas in an Indiana suburb of Chicago in 1940. The story's hero, Ralphie Parker, spends much of the film trying to wheedle a Daisy Red Ryder BB gun out of his parents for Christmas. In addition to the obligatory retort by any adult within earshot, "You'll shoot your eye out!" there is a daydream sequence in which Ralphie fights it out with desperados dressed in black. Of course, in the end, Ralphie's shot ricochets back into his face due to an unsafe choice of targets, making him think that he did, in fact, shoot his eye out.

Besides the Red Ryder, other BB guns were made celebrating western stars, fictional and otherwise—The Lone Ranger, Buffalo Bill, and Annie Oakley. With these guns, and the plainer guns with no radio or historical association, several generations of American children played their games of adventure and, in some cases, mayhem. Over the last twenty years, though, a cultural shift has taken place. With an even greater percentage of the nation's population living in urban areas, the appreciation of firearms has lessened. This trend has effected these small-caliber, low-velocity firearms.

Many of the best and safest arms manufactured by the modern firearms industry are air rifles. Yet the market has been forced to struggle with the backlash from school shootings, violence on television and in movies, and a new generation of parents who never experienced shooting a BB gun with their own parents. Despite this, many companies still produce air rifles. While a number of companies have returned to the Red Ryder style or other "Western"-looking guns to attract beginners (and grandparents), a number of companies make rifles for collegiate and Olympic competition that resemble futuristic ray guns more than air guns. As with Schuetzen rifles and Creedmoor rifles from the 1800s, today's competition air rifles have developed from relatively simple arms developed from military- or Schuetzen-styled rifles to highly machined works of art that provide the shooter with astounding levels of accuracy. As opposed to the $30 to $50 for a "child's" rifle one would find at a discount store, rifles built for serious competition often cost several thousand dollars.

Compared to the air guns of 200 years ago, much less 50 years ago, today's air guns are miracles of engineering. The engineering is not the main attraction to the youth that learn to shoot using these guns, though. As in their grandparents' day, the draw is in the imagination, the fun, the responsibility, and the time spent with parents and friends. The thrill of hitting the bulls-eye on a target and the joy that comes from playacting that you and your friends are great adventurers are simply two aspects of the benefits that many Americans received by learning about guns firsthand from air rifles. The lessons learned were different than those learned manipulating a videogame controller. While many youth play electronic games involving guns, the similarities stop there. The child taught to shoot a real air rifle learns responsibility for actions, dedication to practice, and attention to safety and surroundings. The child learning to shoot any of the dozens of firearms constructed in computer code learns nothing of this, not even how to use their imagination.

MODERN HUNTING ARMS

WINCHESTER AND REMINGTON BOLT ACTION RIFLES

One of the easiest ways to get a fight started in some parts of the modern West is to start up a conversation on hunting rifles. With the variety of makes, models, and calibers, it is hard to choose the "best" gun sometimes. It is also no surprise that many hunters have their favorite gun—and are more than happy to inform others of their preference. While much of this preference is based on experience—with firearms, with hunting, and with shooting in general—this preference often becomes a key part of the hunter's personality.

The reasons behind the importance of this preference lie in the continued importance of the rifle in Western life. While much of the American West is considered settled and "civilized", there are many rural areas in which hunting is not only a form of recreation. In this modern version of the "Wild West", the rural population still relies indirectly, and often directly, on the right to hunt big game. The livelihood of many areas is supported financially by federal excise taxes on firearms and ammunition and the local business generated by hunters.

However, the financial benefits are secondary to many families who still rely on the ability to hunt in order to put food on the table. This is increasingly important as the relationship of income to cost-of-living worsens in many of these areas. For many citizens of the West, a quality rifle changes this equation for the better. Two of the rifles of the 20th

Modern American Hunting Rifles manufactured by Winchester and Remington

century, the Winchester Model 70 and the Remington Model 700, are still the preferred rifles amongst many of these modern residents of the West.

The Winchester Model 70, an upgraded version of the Model 54 by this manufacturer, is considered by many to be the classic bolt-action rifle of the Western hunter. Based on the same design used in the German Mauser rifle and the US Model 1903, and starting production in 1936, this rifle is the standard by which all other hunting rifles are compared. More accurately, the pre-1964 is the standard. The cause of this is a corporate shakeup that occurred in 1963. One result of this shakeup was the belief that cost-cutting in the design, materials, and construction technique for any product could lead to a similar product with higher revenues. Unfortunately for Winchester, the changes turned the industry standard into the firearm equivalent of the Edsel. The changed Model 70 (and many other Winchester products) was much maligned by the users of the new rifle. The disappointment in the redesigned rifle led many shooters to look for another rifle.

The rifle adopted by many of these shooters was the Remington Model 700, which was first introduced in 1962 and soon capitalized on the widespread disdain toward the recent changes in the Model 70. The success of this model was a result of the high quality and accuracy of this rifle compared with the reasonable price of this well-made firearm. During the 1960's and 1970's, many new shooters and former Winchester shooters would use this rifle as "their" rifle. As a result of the various capabilities of this rifle, the United States Marine Corps adopted a modified version of this rifle as their standard sniper firearm during the Vietnam War, replacing the venerable US Model 1903.

Over the last decade, these two rifles have become more equal in the eyes of their users. The quality of the various Winchester firearms has returned to what it once was and Remington has continued to improve their products. This has become very important over the last several decades as many other companies have begun to prove a serious challenge to these manufacturers. All of these companies, using a combination of technologies from the 19th and 21st centuries, are regardless continuing to manufacture rifles that are the successors to the Hawken, the Sharps, and the Winchester lever action. They are allowing hunters to continue to share the experiences of their ancestors and, oftentimes, make sure that there is food on the table.

The choice of a rifle is a personal one. Sometimes it is based on research. Sometimes it is based in observations from friends. And sometimes the reason is simply, "It's what my dad used." The use of a rifle to hunt wild game is one of the only means we now have to relive the lives of our ancestors and one of the only means by which we can provide for ourselves and our families in such a direct manner.

Modern American Hunting Rifles manufactured by Winchester and Remington

GLOSSARY OF FIREARMS TERMINOLOGY

The following glossary is neither a complete or exhaustive treatment of firearms terminology; rather it is meant to be a resource for those gaining familiarity with firearms.

ACTION: A firearm's receiver, bolt (or breech block), loading and firing mechanisms.
AUTOMATIC: A repeating firearm that automatically chambers and fires continuously with a single and sustained pull of the trigger; a machine gun.
AIRGUN: A gun that discharges a pellet or BB by compressed air or gas (typically CO2).
ASSAULT RIFLE: A military/law enforcement type firearm designed to provide either semi-automatic or fully-automatic fire.
BACKSTRAP: The rear part of a pistol's grip frame.
BALLISTICS: The study of the physics of the performance of projectiles, and the prediction and analysis of such performance.
BARREL: A tube through which a projectile passes as it is discharged from a firearm.
BLACK POWDER: An explosive compound (a mixture of charcoal, sulfur, and saltpeter) used for ignition and propulsion in firearms. Black powder is still in use. (See Smokeless Powder.)
BLUING: A finish created by the controlled application of chemical solutions that oxidize the metal surfaces of firearms.
BOLT: A sliding metal bar that seats and removes a cartridge and closes the breech.
BORE: The internal opening of a barrel through which the projectile travels prior to departing the muzzle.
BREECH: The rear section of the barrel of a firearm.
BREECH LOADER: A firearm that is loaded through the rear portion of the barrel.
BUCKHORN SIGHT: A rear, open-topped sight displaying curved sides.
BULL BARREL: A very heavy barrel for use in precision-shooting firearms.
BUTT: The thick end of a stock. (See Stock.)
BUTTPLATE: A metal or synthetic plate covering the rear of the stock.
CALIBER: The interior diameter of the bore of a gun barrel between the lands of the rifling; measured in inches or millimeters.
CARBINE: A rifle with a short barrel originally designed for use from horseback.
CARTRIDGE: A cylinder of metal or other material containing a powder charge, a projectile, and a primer for use in a firearm.
CENTERFIRE CARTRIDGE: A cartridge that has its primer set in the center of the base of its case.
CHAMBER: The enlarged rear portion at the breech end of the barrel that accepts a cartridge.
CHECKERING: Crosshatched lines that are cut into some pistol grips and stocks providing a gripping surface and an ornamental design.
CHOKE: The constricted end of a shotgun barrel that condenses the shot spread.
CLIP: A metal device that holds a series of cartridges so they can be inserted into a magazine.
This term is often misused to mean a detachable magazine. (See Magazine.)
COLOR CASE HARDENING: A heat-treating process that hardens steel and iron and leaves a colorful surface finish.
CROWNING: The relieved (rounded or sunken) muzzle end of a barrel that protects the mouth of the bore.
CYLINDER: A round container that holds a revolver's cartridges in separate chambers and rotates on a pin.
DAMASCUS BARREL: A barrel produced by forging and joining different types of metal strips together. (Also called a "laminated" or "twist" barrel.)
DERRINGER: Usually a small single- or double-barreled pistol meant for concealment. (Also spelled deringer.)

DOUBLE-ACTION: A revolver or semi-automatic pistol function that enables the hammer to be cocked and released by pulling the trigger.

DOUBLE-SET TRIGGER: A mechanism that provides two triggers—one to set the firing mechanism for release and the other to lightly trip the firing mechanism.

DRY FIRING: Operating the firing mechanism of a firearm without using ammunition.

EXTRACTOR: A device that withdraws empty cases from the chamber of a firearm so they can be thrown clear of the firearm by the ejector.

FIRING PIN: A plunger-like part that strikes the primer of a cartridge.

FLINT LOCK: A firearm ignition system using a small flint that, when struck against a steel frizzen, produces sparks that first ignite the priming powder and then the main powder charge.

FORCING CONE: The rear part of a pistol or rifle chamber that channels the projectile into the barrel.

FRAME: The structure of a firearm to which the barrel, action, and stock (or grip panels) are attached.

FRIZZEN: The part of a flintlock's firing mechanism that is struck by a flint, producing sparks that first ignite the priming powder and then the main powder charge.

GAUGE: The bore diameter of a shotgun based on a formula involving the number of lead balls cast from a pound of lead that would fit in a given bore size.

GRIP: A one- or two-piece handle for a revolver or pistol.

GROOVES: Narrow channels cut in the barrel of a firearm that cause a bullet to spin.

HALF-COCK: Partially cocking a firearm so that the hammer doesn't fall; a safety measure.

HAMMER: A moving part of the firearm that causes the firing pin to strike the cartridge primer.

HANDGUN: A firearm designed to be fired with one hand, such as revolvers, auto-loading pistols, and single-shot firearms.

HANGFIRE: A delay in the discharge of a loaded cartridge after the primer has been struck by the firing pin.

HOLLOWPOINT: A bullet with a cavity in the nose that helps it to expand within the target mass.

LANDS: The elevated spaces between the grooves in the bore of a barrel.

MAGAZINE: A container for holding cartridges that are forced by spring pressure into position to be fed into the chamber of a firearm. A magazine can be a detachable or non-detachable box-type or tubular. (See Clip.)

MAGNUM: A larger-than-normal cartridge containing more powder than a standard cartridge of the same bullet diameter. The additional powder charge increases bullet velocity.

MATCH LOCK: A very early type of firing mechanism that moves a lighted, wrapped slow match against a priming powder that, in turn, ignites the powder charge.

MISFIRE: When a cartridge fails to ignite and discharge a projectile. (See Hangfire.)

MUSKET: A long-barreled, smoothbore firearm often of military design.

MUSKETOON: A muzzle-loading, smoothbore carbine.

MUZZLE: The forward end of a barrel where a fired bullet exits.

MUZZLE BRAKE: A device attached to the muzzle of a barrel to reduce recoil.

MUZZLE ENERGY: The energy of a bullet as it exits the muzzle; measured in foot pounds.

MUZZLE LOADER: A firearm with a solid breech that is loaded through the muzzle end of the barrel.

OPEN SIGHT: A notched, open-topped rear sight or an exposed front sight of some configuration.

OVER AND UNDER: One barrel placed on top of the other. Generally a shotgun design, but can be a rifle or rifle/shotgun combination.

PARKERIZING: A dull gray or green gun finish that resists rust. Frequently used on military firearms.

PEEP SIGHT: A rear sight containing a hole through which to line up the front sight and target. (Also called an aperture sight.)

PERCUSSION LOCK: A firing device employing a hammer that strikes a percussion cap containing a detonating compound that ignites the main powder charge.

PRIMERS: Small metallic caps containing an explosive compound that, when struck by a firing pin, ignite the powder charge in a cartridge.

RECEIVER: The section of a rifle or shotgun that houses the action. (See Action.)

REVOLVER: A firearm with a multi-chambered, revolving cylinder and, generally, one barrel. The same principle was used in some early rifles and shotguns.

RIB: An elongated, flat, raised stiffening device attached to a barrel. It can also be a sighting plane or sight base or merely a decorative device.

RIFLE: A long-barreled firearm with a rifled bore.

RIFLING: Spiral grooves cut inside a gun barrel that force a projectile to spin around its longitudinal axis to increase its stability in flight.

RIMFIRE: A cartridge that contains its primer inside the rim of the base of the case.

SAFETY: A mechanism that helps to prevent the discharge of a firearm.

SEAR: The pivoting part of the firing mechanism of a gun that connects the trigger to the hammer or striker and holds it in the cocked position until the trigger is pressed and the gun is fired.

SEMIAUTOMATIC: A repeating firearm that has an automatic chambering mechanism but requires a separate trigger pull for each round fired.

SEMI-WADCUTTER: A truncated bullet with a flat tip.

SHOT: Round lead (or other metal alloys) balls loaded into shotgun shells. The two main divisions of shot: Birdshot–small shot (less than .24 inches); and Buckshot–heavy shot (.24 inches or larger).

SHOTGUN: A firearm with a smooth bore designed for firing a shot-shell containing a charge of small shot at relatively short ranges.

SIDE-BY-SIDE: A twin-barreled shotgun that has its barrels mounted horizontally. Can also be a double rifle or rifle/shotgun combination design.

SINGLE ACTION: A firearm that requires its hammer manually be cocked each time before the trigger can be pulled.

SMOKELESS POWDER: A fast-burning, more stable (than black powder), and more easily ignited powder that burns efficiently without the presence of external oxygen. (See Black Powder.)

STOCK: A wooden, metal, or synthetic part of a long gun that is held by the shooter and is connected to the frame or receiver.

TAKE DOWN: A firearm designed to be disassembled readily into two or more sections for ease of carrying, storage, or shipping.

TANG: The upper and lower metal prongs of a long gun that connect the frame or receiver to the stock.

TELESCOPIC SIGHT: An optical sight attached to a firearm that magnifies the shooter's view of a target.

TOP STRAP: The upper part (above the cylinder) of a revolver frame.

TRAJECTORY: The flight path of a bullet after it leaves the barrel.

TRIGGER: A mechanism that initiates the firing of a gun.

WADCUTTER: A target-shooting bullet that has a completely flat point that cuts a clean hole in a paper target.

WHEEL LOCK: A spring-activated steel mechanism that spins a serrated wheel against a piece of pyrite or other mineral creating sparks that ignite the priming charge, which then flashes through to ignite the propellant powder charge.

WILDCAT CARTRIDGE: A non-standard cartridge made by a noncommercial producer.

FIREARMS BIBLIOGRAPHY

GENERAL REFERENCE AND HISTORIES

Barnes, Frank C. *Cartridges of the World, 10th Edition.* Edited by Stan Skinner. Iola, WI: Krause Publications, 2003.

Blackmore, Howard. *Guns and Rifles of the World.* New York: Viking Press, 1965.

Bogdanovic, Branko, & Valencak, Ivan. *The Great Century of Guns.* New York: Gallery Guns, 1986.

Ezell, Edward C. *Small Arms of the World. 12th Edition.* Harrisburg, PA: Stackpole Books, 1983.

Flayderman, Norm. *Flayderman's Guide to Antique American Firearms and Their Values, 8th edition.* Northbrook, IL: Krause Publications.

Greener, W.W. *The Gun and Its Development.* Secaucus, NJ: Chartwell Books, 1988.

Hogg, Ian. *The Complete Illustrated Encyclopedia of the World's Firearms.* New York: A & W Publishers, 1978.

Hogg, Ian. *Handguns and Rifles: The Finest Weapons from Around the World.* London: Lyons Press, 1997.

Fadala, Sam. *The Complete Black Powder Handbook, 4th Edition.* Iola, WI: Krause Publications, 2001.

Fjestad, S.P. *Blue Book of Gun Values.* (Updated once a year.) Minneapolis, MN: Blue Book Publishing.

Krasne, Jerry A. *Encyclopedia and Reference Catalog for Auto Loading Guns.* San Diego, CA: Triple K Manufacturing, 1989.

Mathews, J. Howard. *Firearms Identification.* (Three volume set.) Springfield, IL: Charles C.

Thomas, 1973. (First printed in 1962.) Philip, Craig, *The World's Great Small Arms.* New York: Barnes and Noble, 1993.

Schwing, Ned. *Standard Catalog of Firearms.* (the latest version.) Iola, WI: Krause Publications.

Serven, James E. *200 Years of American Firearms.* Chicago: Follett Publishing Company, 1975.

The Diagram Group. *Weapons: An International Encyclopedia from 5000 BC to 2000 AD.* New York: St. Martin's Press, 1990.

Walter, John. *Rifles of the World. 2nd Edition.* Iola, WI: Krause Publications, 1998.

Walter, John. *Dictionary of Guns and Gunmakers.* Mechanicsburg, PA: Stackpole Books, 2001.

Walter, John. *The Guns that Won the West: Firearms on the American Frontier, 1848–1898.* Mechanicsburg, PA: Stackpole Books, 1999.

Wilson, R.L. *Silk and Steel: Women at Arms.* New York: Random House, 2003.

AIRGUNS

Beeman, Robert Dr. and Allen, John. *Blue Book of Airguns.* (the most current edition.) Minneapolis, MN: Blue Book Publications.

Hoff, Arne. *Airguns and Other Pneumatic Arms.* London: Barrier & Jenkins, 1972.

House, James E. *American Air Rifles.* Iola, WI: Krause Publications, 2001.

House, James E. *CO2 Pistols and Rifles.* Iola, WI: Krause Publications, 2003.

BALLARD

Dutcher, John T. *Ballard: The Great American Single Shot Rifle.* Denver: Published by author, 2002.

West, Bill. *Marlin and Ballard Firearms History.* Norwalk, CA: Stockton Trade Press, 1977.

BROWNING

Browning, John & Gentry, Curt. *John M. Browning: American Gunmaker. An Illustrated Biography of the Man and His Guns.* Garden City, NY: Double Day, 1964.

Eastman, Matt. *Browning Sporting Arms of Distinction 1903–1992.* Long Beach, CA: Safari Press, 1994.

Ratenbury, Richard. *The Browning Connection: Patent Prototypes in the Winchester Museum.* Cody, WY: Buffalo Bill Historical Center, 1982.

Schwing, Ned. *The Browning Superimposed: John Browning's Last Legacy.* Iola, WI: Krause Publications, 1996.

Stevens, R. *The Browning High Power Automatic Pistol.* Toronto: Collector Grade Publications, 1990.

West, Bill. *Browning Arms and History.* Santa Fe Springs, CA: Stockton Trade Press, Inc., 1972.

Vanderlinden, Anthony. *Belgian Browning Pistols 1889–1949.* Greensboro, NC: Wet Dog Publications, 2001.

Vanderlinden, Anthony & Shirley, H.M. *Browning Auto-5 Shotgun—The Belgian Production.* Greensboro, NC: Wet Dog Publications, 2003.

COLT

A Century of Achievement: 1836–1936. Hartford, CT: Colt's Patent Firearms Manufacturing Company, 1936.

Bady, David B. *Colt Automatic Pistols.* Los Angeles: Borden Publishing Company, 1973.

Boorman, Dean K. *The History of Colt Firearms.* New York: The Lyons Press, 2001.

Breslin, John D. et al. *Variations of Colt's: New Model Police & Pocket Breech Loading Pistols.* Lincoln, RI: Andrew Mowbray Publishers, 2002.

Cochran, Keith. *Colt Peacemaker Encyclopedia. Volumes 1 & 2.* Rapid City, SD: Cochran Publishing Company, 1992 & 1998.

Grant, Elsworth S. *The Colt Armory: A History of Colt's Manufacturing Company, Inc.* Lincoln, RI: Mowbray Publishing, 1995.

Haven, Charles & Beldon, Frank. *A History of the Colt Revolver and the Other Arms Made by Colt's Patent Firearms Manufacturing Company from 1836 to 1940.* New York: Bonanza Books, 1978 (first published in 1940).

Kopec, Graham, and Moore. *A Study of the Colt Single Action Army Revolver.* Dallas: Taylor Publishing, 1978.

McDowell, R. *A Study of Colt Conversions and Other Percussion Revolvers.* Iola, WI: Krause Publications, 1997.

Roes, K.T., editor. *Colt and Its Collectors: Exhibition Catalog for Colt: Legacy of a Legend, Buffalo Bill Historical Center.* Cody, WY: Wordsworth Publishing, 2003.

Tivey, T. *The Colt Rifle, 1884–1902.* NSW Australia: Couston and Hall, 1984.

Wilson, R.L. *Colt, An American Legend.* New York: Abbeville Press, 1989.

Wilson, R.L. *The Book of Colt Firearms.* Minneapolis, MN: Blue Book Publications, Inc., 1993.

Wilkerson, Don. *Colt Single Action Army Revolver, Pre-War/Post-War Model.* Minneapolis, MN: Broughton Printing, Inc., 1991.

HIGH STANDARD

Dance, Tom. *High Standard: A Collector's Guide to the Hamden and Hartford Target Pistols.* Lincoln, RI: Andrew Mowbray Publishers, 1991.

Petty, Charles, E. *High Standard Automatic Pistols 1932–1950.* Highland Park, NJ: The Gun Room Press, 1989.

L.C. SMITH

Brophy, William S. *L.C. Smith Shotguns.* North Hollywood, CA: Beinfeld Publishing Company, 1977.

Brophy, William S. *Plans and Specifications of the L. C. Smith Shotguns.* Montezuma, IA: F. Brownell, 1981.

MARLIN

Brophy, William S. *Marlin Firearms: A History of the Guns and the Company that Made Them.* Mechanicsburg, PA: Stackpole Books, 1989.

Kenna, Frank. *The Marlin Story.* New York: Newcomen Society in North America, 1975.

West, Bill. *Marlin and Ballard Firearms History.* Norwalk, CA: Stockton Trade Press, Inc., 1977.

PARKER

Baer, Larry L. *The Parker Book.* North Hollywood, CA: Beinfeld Publishing Company, 1974.

Baer, Larry L. *The Parker Gun.* Los Angeles, CA: Beinfeld Publications, 1980.

Gunther, Mullins, et al. *The Parker Story.* (Volumes 1 & 2) Knoxville, TN: Parker Joint Venture Group, 1998 & 2000.

Muderlak, Ed. *Parker Guns: The "Old Reliable."* Long Beach, CA: Safari Press, 1997.

Price, Charlie & Parker Story Joint Venture Group. *Parker Gun Identification and Serialization.* Minneapolis, MN: Blue Book Publications, Inc., 2002.

REMINGTON

A New Chapter in an Old Story. New York: Remington Arms-Union Metallic Cartridge Company, 1912.

Ball, Robert. *Remington Firearms: The Golden Age of Collecting.* Iola, WI: Krause Publications, 1995.

Hatch, Alden. *Remington Arms in American History.* New York: Rinehart, 1956.

Karr, C.L. & Karr C.R. *Remington Handguns.* Harrisburg, PA: Stackpole Company, 1956.

Kirkland, K.D. *America's Premier Gunmaker, Remington.* New York: Exeter Books, 1988.

Madaus, Howard & Simeon Stoddard. *The Guns of Remington: Historic Firearms Spanning Two Centuries.* Dayton, KY: Biplane Productions, 1997.

Marcot, Roy. *Remington, America's Oldest Gunmaker.* Peoria, IL: Primedia Special Interest Publications, 1998.

Schreier, Konrad F. *Remington Rolling Block Firearms.* Union City, TN: Pioneer Press, 1977.
Semmer, Charles G. *Remington Double Shotguns.* Denver: Published by author, 1997.
Trout, Douglas. *Remington Arms Company, Inc.* Ilion, New York. U.S. Department of Health and Human Services, 1997.
West, Bill. *Remington Arms & History.* Whittier, CA: Stockton Trade Press, Inc., 1970.

RUGER

Hiddleson, C. *Encyclopedia of Ruger Semi-Automatic Pistols: 1949–1992.* Iola, WI: Krause Publications, 1993.
Wilson, R.L. *Ruger and His Guns.* New York: Simon and Schuster, 1996.
Workman, W.E. *The Ruger 10/22.* Iola, WI: Krause Publications, 1994.

SAVAGE/STEVENS

Murray, Douglas P. *The Ninety-Nine: A History of the Savage Model 99 Rifle.* Published by author, 2000.
Cope, K.L. Stevens *Pistols and Pocket Rifles.* Ottawa, Ontario: Museum Restoration Service, 1971.
Kimmel, J. *Savage and Stevens Arms Collector's History.* Portland, OR: Corey/Stevens Publishing, Inc., 1990.
West, Bill. *Savage and Stevens Arms and History.* Whittier, CA: Stockton Trade Press, Inc., 1971.

SHARPS

Sellers, Frank. *Sharps Firearms.* North Hollywood: Beinfeld Publishing Company, 1978.
Smith, Winston O. *The Sharps Rifle, Its History, Development and Operation.* New York: W. Morrow and Company, 1943.
Wiley, Sword. *Hiram Berdan, His Famous Sharpshooters, and Their Sharps Rifles.* Lincoln, RI: A. Mowbray, 1988.

SMITH & WESSON

Boorman, Dean. *The History of Smith & Wesson Firearms.* Guilford, CT: The Lyons Press, 2002.
Jinks, Roy G. *Artistry in Arms: The Guns of Smith & Wesson.* Springfield, MA: Smith & Wesson, 1992.
Jinks, Roy G. *History of Smith & Wesson: No Thing of Importance Will Come Without Effort.* N. Hollywood, CA: Beinfeld Publishing Company, 1977.
Neal, Robert J. & Jinks, Roy G. *History of Smith and Wesson.* North Hollywood, CA: Beinfeld Publishing, Inc., 1977.
Supica, Jim & Nahas, Richard. *Standard Catalog of Smith & Wesson.* 2nd edition. Iola, WI: Krause Publications, 2001.

WINCHESTER

Boorman, Dean K. *The History of Winchester Firearms.* New York: Lyons Press, 2001.
Henshaw, Thomas, editor. *The History of Winchester Firearms, 1866–1992.* 6th Edition. New York: The Winchester Press, 1993.
Houze, Herbert G. *Winchester Bolt Action Military and Sporting Rifles, 1877–1937.* Lincoln, RI: Andrew Mowbray Publishers, 1998.
Houze, Herbert G. *Winchester Repeating Arms Company: Its History and Development From 1865 to 1981.* Iola, WI: Krause Publications, 1994.
Kowalski, David D., editor. *Standard Catalog of Winchester: The Most Comprehensive Price Guide Ever Published.* Iola, WI: 2000.
Madis, George. *The Winchester Book.* Brownsboro, TX: Art and Reference House, 1985.
Madis, George. *The Winchester Handbook.* Ann Arbor, MI: Edwards Brothers, 1981.
MS 20: Winchester Repeating Arms Company Files. McCracken Research Library, Buffalo Bill Historical Center, Cody, WY. (Archives of the Winchester Repeating Arms Company.)
Trolard, Tom. *Winchester Commemoratives.* Coos Bay, OR: Commemorative Guns, 1985.
Watrous, George R. et al. *The History of Winchester Firearms 1865 to 1975. 4th edition.* New York: The Winchester Press, 1975.
Webster, Tom. *Winchester Rarities.* Edited by David D. Kowalski. Iola, WI: Krause Publications, 2000.
Wilson, R.L. *Winchester: An American Legend: The Official History of Winchester Firearms and Ammunition from 1849 to the Present.* New York: Random House, 1991.
Winchester Repeating Arms Catalogs. 12 reprinted volumes (1865–1918). Oceanside, CA: Armory Publications, 1991–1992.

MILITARY

Ball, Robert. *Mauser Military Rifles of the World.* Iola, WI: Krause Publications, 1996.

Brophy, William S. *The Krag Rifle.* Los Angeles, CA: Beinfeld Publications, 1980.

Canfield, Bruce N. *The Winchester in the Service.* Lincoln, RI: Andrew Mowbray Publishers, 1991.

Canfield, Bruce N. *U.S. Infantry Weapons of World War II.* Lincoln, RI: Andrew Mobrey Publishers, 1994.

Coggins, Jack. *Arms and Equipment of the Civil War.* New York: Doubleday, 1962.

Hammer, Kenneth M. *The Springfield Carbine on the Western Frontier (Revised).* Bozeman, MT: Little Buffalo Press, 2002.

Hogg, Ian V. and Weeks, John. *Military Small Arms of the 20th century. 5th edition.* Northfield, IL: DBI Books, 1985.

Honeycutt, Fred L., Jr. *Military Pistols of Japan.* Lake Park, FL: Julin Books, 1982.

Hopkins, Richard E. *Military Sharps Rifles and Carbines.* Campbell, CA: Published by author, 1967.

Kirk, J. and Young, Robert. *Great Weapons of World War II.* New York: Young, Walker and Company, 1961.

Markham, George. *Japanese Infantry Weapons of World War Two.* New York: Hippocrene Books, Inc., 1976.

Moller, G.D. *American Military Shoulder Arms, Volumes 1 & 2.* Niwot, CO: University Press of Colorado, 1993.

Peterson, H.L. *Arms and Armor in Colonial America.* New York: Brandall House, 1956.

Poyer, Joe and Riesch, Craig. *The .45-70 Springfield.* Tustin, CA: North Cape Publication, 1999.

Reilly, R. *United States Military Small Arms 1816–1865.* Baton Rouge, LA: Eagle Press, Inc., 1970.

Reuland, Walter P. *Cartridges for the Springfield Trapdoor Rifles & Carbines, 1865–1898.* Laramie, WY: Heritage Concepts, 1993.

Schwing, Ned. *Standard Catalog of Military Firearms.* (the latest version.) Iola, WI: Krause Publications.

Skennerton, Ian. *British Small Arms of World War II.* Labrador, Australia: Published by author, 1988.

Still, Jan C. *Axis Pistols.* Marceline, MO: Walsworth Publishing Company, 1991.

Still, Jan C. *Third Reich Lugers.* Marceline, MO: Walsworth Publishing Company, 1988.

Waite, M.D. et al. *Trapdoor Springfield: The United States Springfield Single-Shot Rifle, 1865–1898.* North Hollywood, CA: Beinfeld Publishing, 1980.

Walter, John. *Modern Military Rifles.* Mechanicsburg, PA: Stackpole Books, 2001.

FIREARMS CARE AND MAINTENANCE

Angier, R.H. *Firearms Blueing and Browning.* Mechanicsburg, PA: Stackpole Books, 1936.

Newell, A. Donald. *Gunstock Finishing and Care.* Mechanicsburg, PA: Stackpole Books, 1949.

Traister, John E. *Professional Care and Finishing of Gun Metal.* Blue Ridge Summit, PA: TAB Books, Inc., 1982.

Wood, J.B. *Firearms Assembly/Disassembly: Parts I thru V.* Northfield, IL: DBI Books, various years.

Wood, J.B. *The Gun Digest of Gun Care, Cleaning & Refinishing: Book One and Book Two.* Northfield, IL: DBI Books, 1984 –1985.

SOURCES FOR GLOSSARY:

Fjestad, S.P. *24th Edition Blue Book of Gun Values.* Minneapolis, MN: Blue Book Publications, 2003.

Markowitz, David S. *A Glossary of Firearms Terminology v1.6.1.* Copyright c. 1996-98 Josh Markowitz. http://www.building-tux.com/dsmjd/tech/glossary.htm.(Accessed July 23, 2004.)

Mueller, Chester and Olson, John. *Small Arms Lexicon and Concise Encyclopedia.* South Hackensack, NJ: Shooter's Bible, Inc., 1968.

National Rifle Association. *Firearms Glossary.* Copyright 2004, National Rifle Association of America, Institute for Legislative Action.

http://www.nraila.org/issues/FireArmsGlossary/Default.aspx Newman, Warren.

Basic Glossary of Firearms Terminology. Cody, WY: Cody Firearms Museum, Buffalo Bill Historical Center, undated.

Nonte, George C., Jr. *Firearms Encyclopedia.* New York: Harper & Row, 1973 (reprinted 1978).

PHOTO CREDITS

All objects and historical photographs, except the front cover firearm, are from the collections of the Buffalo Bill Historical Center, Cody, Wyoming. Photographs of objects are by Bruce Curtis except where noted.

Cover photographs: Gun photograph by Bruce Curtis. Front and back cover photographic portraits are from the collection of the Buffalo Bill Historical Center. Left top: Portrait of Alexander Phimister Proctor, Gift of Phimister and Sally Church; P.242.2. Left bottom: Portrait of William F. Cody, P.69.920. Back cover: Portrait of Geronimo,Vincent Mercaldo Collection; P.71.643.2.

pp. 3–4: Historical images from the collection of the Buffalo Bill Historical Center
pp. 12–14: Kenneth R. Lennington Collection; 1997.6.1
pp. 15–16: Gift of Brian P. and Ann A. McDonald; 1999.22.13
pp. 17–18: Gift of Olin Corporation, Winchester Arms Collection; 1988.8.1328
p. 20: Gift of Olin Corporation, Winchester Arms Collection; 1988.8.1584
p. 22: Gift of F. W. Roebling, III; 2000.14.1
p. 24: Photograph from the collection of the Buffalo Bill Historical Center. Gift of F. W. Roebling, III; 2000.14.1 (rifle), 2000.14.2.1 (knife), 2000.14.2.2 (scabbard); photo mount designed by Doogie Horner.
p. 25: Photograph from the collection of the Buffalo Bill Historical Center, P.69.1276
p. 28: Gift of Olin Corporation, Winchester Arms Collection; 1988.8.2111, 1988.8.2121
p. 29: Gift of Olin Corporation, Winchester Arms Collection; 1988.8.2113, 1988.8.2108
p. 30: Photograph from the collection of the Buffalo Bill Historical Center, Gift of Phimister and Sally Church; P.242.2
p. 32 (left): Photograph from the collection of the Buffalo Bill Historical Center, Gift of the Gordon T. Matson Family; 1996.12.1
p. 32 (right): Photograph from the collection of the Buffalo Bill Historical Center, Vincent Mercaldo Collection; P.71.643.2
p. 34: Gift of Olin Corporation, Winchester Arms Collection; 1988.8.779
p. 37: Gift of Olin Corporation, Winchester Arms Collection; 1988.8.1673
p. 39: Gift of Olin Corporation, Winchester Arms Collection; 1988.8.761, photo mount designed by Doogie Horner.
p. 40: Gift of Olin Corporation, Winchester Arms Collection; 1988.8.2241
p. 41: Gift of Olin Corporation, Winchester Arms Collection; 1988.8.761
p. 42: Gift of Olin Corporation, Winchester Arms Collection; 1988.8.2524 (bottom), 1988.8.2521 (top)
p. 43: Gift of Olin Corporation, Winchester Arms Collection; 1988.8.2524
p. 45: Photograph from the collection of the Buffalo Bill Historical Center, Vincent Mercaldo Collection; P.71.1632.1
pp. 48–49: Gift of Olin Corporation, Winchester Arms Collection; 1988.8.1795
p. 51: Gift of Patricia Trowbridge; 1992.5.13
p. 54: Photograph from the collection of the Buffalo Bill Historical Center, Vincent Mercaldo Collection; P.71.1925.3
p. 55: Gift of Olin Corporation, Winchester Arms Collection; 1988.8.735
p. 57: Gift of Olin Corporation, Winchester Arms Collection; 1988.8.2792, 1988.8.2780
p. 59: Gift of Olin Corporation, Winchester Arms Collection; 1988.8.1330
p. 61: Vincent Mercaldo Collection; P.71.355
p. 64: 1983.7.1, photo mount designed by Doogie Horner.
p. 65: 1983.7.1
p. 67: Gift of Richard and Jan Wasson in memory of our son, Stuart England Wasson; 2003.16.1
p. 69: Gift of Mr. William Fahnestock, Jr.; 1.69.2179
p. 71: Gift of Sanford D. Beecher; 1.69.2219
p. 74: Gift of Olin Corporation, Winchester Arms Collection; 1988.8.464, 1988.8.1163
p. 75: Gift of Olin Corporation, Winchester Arms Collection; 1988.8.1163
p. 76 (top): Gift of Olin Corporation, Winchester Arms Collection; 1988.8.464; (bottom): Detail of photograph from the collection of the Buffalo Bill Historical Center, P.71.1983.1
p. 78: Gift of A. W. Lusthoff; 1991.7.1

p. 80: Gift in memory of James R. Kilborn Sr., 1902-1972, by his son, James R. Kilborn Jr., Allenwood, PA; 2002.19.1
pp. 84–85: Gift in the memory of a good friend, William B. Ruger, Sr.; 2002.10.1
p. 87: Gifted by the Tobin Family in loving memory of John H. Tobin; 2003.10.1
p. 88: Gift of Olin Corporation, Winchester Arms Collection; 1988.8.1329
p. 89: Gift of Olin Corporation, Winchester Arms Collection; 1988.8.1329, photo mount designed by Doogie Horner
p. 91: Photograph from the collection of the Buffalo Bill Historical Center, Gift of Olin Corporation, Winchester Arms Collection; 1988.8.3283
pp. 93–94: 1984.2.1
p. 96: Gift of Olin Corporation, Winchester Arms Collection; 1988.8.181
pp. 98 & 100: Gift of Olin Corporation, Winchester Arms Collection; 1988.8.187
p. 101: Photograph from the collection of the Buffalo Bill Historical Center, P.69.3
p. 104: Photograph from the collection of the Buffalo Bill Historical Center, P.69.920
p. 105: Photograph from the collection of the Buffalo Bill Historical Center, P.69.30
p. 106: Photograph from the collection of the Buffalo Bill Historical Center, P.69.1800
p. 107: Photograph from the collection of the Buffalo Bill Historical Center, P.6.906
p.108: Photograph from the collection of the Buffalo Bill Historical Center, Vincent Mercaldo Collection; P.71.59
p. 110: 1.69.25
p. 111: Photograph from the collection of the Buffalo Bill Historical Center, Vincent Mercaldo Collection; P.71.351
p. 112: Portrait photograph from the collection of the Buffalo Bill Historical Center, Vincent Mercaldo Collection; P.71.362. Rifle: Gift of Dorothy Stone Collins; 1.69.25
p. 114: Photograph from the collection of the Buffalo Bill Historical Center, Gift of The Coe Foundation; 1.67.335
p. 115: Gift of The Coe Foundation; 1.67.335
p. 117: Gift of Olin Corporation, Winchester Arms Collection; 1988.8.1880
pp. 119–120: Donated in Loving Memory of Robert Jesse Moore by his family; 1991.1.1
p. 122: Gift of Mr. and Mrs. Walter Karabian; 1982.4.1
p. 124: Gift from Dr. Lynn Parsons and Dr. Jerry Parsons in memory of their father, Herbert Parsons; 2003.15.16
p. 125: Gift of Olin Corporation, Winchester Arms Collection; 1988.8.1328
p. 128: Gift of Larry and Betty Lou Sheerin; 2004.20.1; Gift of Olin Corporation, Winchester Arms Collection; 1988.8.2798, 1988.8.2794, 1988.8.2793, 1988.8.2767, 1988.8.2753
p. 131: Gift of Mrs. Margaret S. Garlow; 1.69.2262
p. 133: Donated by Tom Blankenship in memory of his uncle, George Heller; 1994.25.1
p. 135: Gift in memory of James C. Mole; 2004.4.1
p. 137: Gift of the Honorable Richard B. Cheney, Vice President of the United States; 2004.3.1, 2004.6.1
p. 139: Gift of Olin Corporation, Winchester Arms Collection; 1988.8.3092, 1988.8.493, 1988.8.446
p. 140: Gift of Olin Corporation, Winchester Arms Collection; 1988.8.3092, 1988.8.446
p. 141: Gift of Olin Corporation, Winchester Arms Collection; 1988.8.3092, 1988.8.493, 1988.8.446
p. 143: Gift of Colt's Manufacturing Company; 2003.20.2
pp. 144–145: Gift of James L. Gallagher; 1991.14.1
p. 146 (top to bottom): Gift of Brian P. and Ann A. McDonald, 1999.22.13 (Girandoni Air Rifle); 1991.5.1 (Lukens Air Rifle); Gift of Thomas K. Hutchinson, 1993.8.60 (Daisy Model 36 Air Rifle)
pp. 149–150: Bequest of the Maurice Albert Postle Estate; 2000.5.8; Gift of Francis Samp; 1998.5.48
pp. 160: Historical images from the collection of the Buffalo Bill Historical Center

CARL LAEMMLE, OFFERS
IE WALCAMP
IN
CODY RIDES WILD
ONE OF THE FAMOUS
SADDLE" STORIES
W. F. "BUFFALO BILL" CO
REWARD
($500.00)
Reward for the capture, dead or alive,
of one Wm. Bonney better known as
"BILLY THE KID"